Issues of New Constitution Making in

Sri Lanka

Towards Ethnic Reconciliation

LAKSIRI FERNANDO

ISBN-13: 978-1539546795
ISBN-10: 1539546799

Published by Createspace
Charleston, SC, USA

DEDICATION

This book is dedicated to the new constitution making process in
Sri Lanka

*"The Constitution doesn't belong to a bunch of judges and lawyers. It belongs to
you."*

-   Anthony Kennedy (US Supreme Court Judge)

CONTENTS

Introduction   VII

Acknowledgements   XV

Abbreviations   XVI

Part I   General Concerns on Constitutional Issues   1

Democratic Dilemma in Sri Lanka

Human Rights and the 1978 Constitution

Why do we need a New Constitution?

Strengthening Horizontal Democracy

Promoting Local Governance

Sri Lanka is Already Quasi Unitary

Federalism, Confederation or Separate State?

Going Beyond the 13-A and Towards Cooperative
Devolution

More Q&A on Devolution

Electoral Reforms should take Equal Priority

**Part II   Proposals to the Public Representation   99
                Committee**

Proposals for a New Constitution

Proposed Chapter on Fundamental Human Rights

Proposed Chapter on Local Government

Part III   **Constitution Making in Perspective**   **137**

Understanding the Political Change in 2015

Balanced Regional Development through Devolution

Civil Society Must Take Over Local Government

Two Dimensions of the National Question

Making a Stop to Acrimonious 'Ethnic Debates'

Building Inter-Ethnic 'Social Capital' for Reconciliation

Selected Bibliography   **186**

INTRODUCTION

This is a collection of essays and articles written and mostly published from time to time covering various issues of constitution making in Sri Lanka. The focus of all of them is ethnic reconciliation. The timing of this publication is the ongoing efforts in Parliament in consultation with the public and various stakeholders in drafting a new constitution and adopting it in Parliament subsequently endorsed by a referendum, according to the constitutional provisions of the present Constitution (1978). Referendum for a new constitution is an important constitutional requirement. Therefore, it should be said at the outset that no 'constitutional revolution' is anticipated in this effort like in 1972.[1] The rationale or the felt need for a new constitution is long standing although this is going to be the fourth constitution of Sri Lanka, if it is successful, since independence in 1948. Admittedly, therefore, there has been some continuous disequilibrium in constitutional matters in the country.

The first constitution or popularly called the Soulbury constitution was primarily a document drafted by the colonial state makers, Lord Soulbury and Sir Ivor Jennings, of course in consultation with the elected

---

[1] It was called a 'constitutional revolution' as it was adopted through a Constituent Assembly outside Parliament going beyond the previous constitution. A. J. Wilson used this term (See 'Sri Lanka Tamil Nationalism, 2000, p. 121).

representatives of the country. However this constitution lasted for 25 years from 1947 to 1972 without much upheaval. In contrast, the first indigenous and the first republican constitution of 1972 survived only for six years. The second republican constitution of 1978 is still in operation for 38 years but largely due to its rigidity than any inherent quality of popular acceptance. Since 1994, there have been several fervent efforts to overhaul it but without any success. In August 2000, the effort to inaugurate a new constitution came very close, but failed, the opposition members of parliament burning the draft agreed by the leaders during by-partisan negotiations.

One advantage of constitution making process today is the existence of a 'national unity' government of the two main political parties, the UNP and the SLFP, also with the connivance of the official opposition, the TNA, representing the Northern Tamil constituency. Therefore, at least on appearance, there seems to be some broad consensus for the need for a new constitution. This could however be illusory, considering the rifts within the 'national unity government' itself on some of the key constitutional issues, and the stance of the almost breakaway Joint Opposition (JO) from the SLFP/UPFA led by the former president, Mahinda Rajapaksa, among other factors. In a recently held 'foot-march' (*Pada Yathra*) of the JO (28 July – 1 August), one of the main slogans was the claim that 'a new constitution is a death trap.' In addition, on the issue of passing the Office on Missing Persons (OMP) Bill, the behavior of the Joint Opposition has heralded what they might do during the inauguration of a new constitution.[2]

There is no single theme or discourse underlying the present publication, except the need for a new constitution reforming many of the institutional and legal anomalies of the present constitutional system, and creating a balance between divergent political views in order that a workable 'constitutional equilibrium' is created for a foreseeable future. This is by no means an easy task. There is no apparent readymade agreement between the main political parties, the UNP, the SLFP, the TNA or the JVP, except the need for a new constitution. What elements could create a sustainable 'constitutional equilibrium' is also not a self-evident matter.

---

[2] *The Island*, see lead stories, 12 and 13 August 2016.

There can be different understandings of what people mean by 'constitutional equilibrium' but here it is mainly used to mean necessary 'political consensuses' for its long term sustainability.[3] A major necessary component in this equilibrium is people's trust in the system. As a US Supreme Court Judge, Anthony Kennedy, has declared, "The Constitution doesn't belong to a bunch of judges and lawyers. It belongs to you." There can be another meaning, not very distance from the above, to mean 'equilibrium between various institutions and power centers.' This is the most traditional interpretation of constitutional equilibrium/disequilibrium. This is about 'checks and balances' not only between the three main branches of government – the legislative, executive and judicial – but also between the provincial governments and the central government.[4] As Sri Lanka is and going to be a devolved system of government, the latter equilibrium is much more important and desired. It could be assumed that if an equilibrium could be achieved in the institutional context, then it would be easy to achieve equilibrium or consensus for sustainability of the constitution system as a whole.

Then what about the trust of the people over the constitutional system? Unless there is a necessary trust, there cannot be a sustainable constitutional equilibrium in the country. This is also called 'constitutional legitimacy.' Wasn't this a reason for two insurrections in the country in the South (1971) and in the North (1983-1987)? I would count the movements after 1987 both in the North and in the South as 'terrorism' and not rebellion or insurrection.

There are three major areas where constitutional consensus or equilibrium is necessary. First or most popular is the question of 'presidential versus a cabinet system.' There has been a long debate on that theme beginning from the initial works of N. M. Perera and A. Jeyaratnam Wilson. Their relevant publications are given in the Bibliography. This may appear the most settled issue particularly after the 19th Amendment, nevertheless there

---

[3] For a similar exposition or meaning see: Adam Lamparello, "Restoring Constitutional Equilibrium," *Social Science Research Network*, December 2013.

[4] The traditional notion of checks and balances was always defended on the basis of constitutional equilibrium since Montesquieu's time. See Colleen Sheehan, *The Mind of James Madison: The Legacy of Classical Republicanism*, Cambridge University Press, 2015.

are several leftover matters, whether all the executive powers should be scrapped from the presidency, and how even a ceremonial president should be elected or selected.

The second is the question of 'proportional representation (PR) versus first-past-the post system (FPP).' This has also been discussed for a long period although not that systematically like the first issue. One reason seems to be the technical matters involved in any electoral discussion and it is not so much of the FPP that is advocated but having a constituency system where the electors having a clear representative to represent them in parliament. Although one objective to advocate initially a quasi FPP system was to have governmental stability through clear majorities, the concerns seem to settle down today as the new thinking accepts the merits of consensual governments instead of one party dominance. The remaining issues seem to point out the necessary balance rather than one against the other.

The third and most controversial today emerges out of the 'unitary versus federal' debate.[5] This has been a never ending dispute in the country linked to the ethnic conflict. Although there is a system of devolution with provincial councils today still there are 'pull factors' wanting to re-establish the old unitary system. On the other hand, there are strong 'push factors' asking for federalism or even beyond, or failing which to properly implement the Thirteenth Amendment or 13A+. What balance of power could be drawn between the central government and the provincial councils would be a key issue. Much of the efforts of the present constitution makers, if not the whole constituent assembly, might be devoted to this issue, given the sensitivity of the matters involved.

There are of course several other polarized issues such as 'secular-state versus foremost place for Buddhism' and the merits and demerits of 'unicameral verses bicameral' legislative system. In most of the above underlined controversial issues, there can be a middle ground which could be achieved, if the parties are willing. However, 'unicameral-bicameral' issue is something a middle position cannot be achieved by the nature of the issue. It has to be either unicameral or bicameral. If a proper and

---

[5] For a strong view against 'federalism' from the South see Dayan Jayatilleka, "Weakening the Centre through Covert Federalism," *Colombo Telegraph*, 1 September 2016.

meaningful devolved system is agreed upon, it is most likely that the constitution might go for a bicameral system. Then the issues would be about the weightage given for the center and the periphery for electing such a second chamber or a senate.

The main premise of the constitutional system in Sri Lanka like in many other democratic countries is the concept of people's sovereignty. What does it mean? Is it only a 'cake decoration' or just a popular slogan to deceive people, while the political elite holding the actual sovereignty? This is not a well debated issue in the country while there have been few attempts. There are of course several devices, apart from the system of elections, which gives the impression that the people are sovereign. One is the provisions for referenda. The other is the constitutional provision for the people to go before the Supreme Court on fundamental rights or to mitigate legislation or executive action which goes against the constitution or its provisions on people's sovereignty through similar legal procedures. Nevertheless, there are limits. The full range of constitutional review is not within the present constitution. Therefore, one can argue that the reinstatement of full judicial review could go a long way in establishing people's sovereignty.

However, the gap between the constitutional system and the people are considerable. The National Youth Survey conducted in 2009 (only survey of this kind) amply revealed that the alienation is quite high in respect of the political, constitutional and the state (institutional) system, particularly among the youth. There have been no direct surveys conducted to gather the opinions of the people on various constitutional questions in the country. The partial observations or studies reveal that the knowledge or opinions of the people are quite low and shrouded in misconceptions. For example, as one constitutional expert has opined, when many people say a 'unitary state' what they mean is a 'united country.' Whether this may be the case or not, the fact remains that the general knowledge on constitutional matters is abysmally low. This is one reason for the continuous imbalance between the constitutional system and the people's aspirations, while the unscrupulous political leaders utilizing the situation for their political ends.

What path the constitution making process should take? What might be the best? The short answer is the Middle Path. The transformation of the present constitutional disequilibrium (and also ambiguities) into sustainable equilibrium is not an easy task. It requires truly a bi-partisan approach. As discussed before, almost all the issues appear to be 'bipolar' due to historical, theoretical, international and political circumstances. At the same time, that nature of the controversies signify the possibility of achieving a middle ground on all or most of the issues, if there is 'political will.' The present national unity government, President Maithripala Sirisena as the head, is in a better position to achieve such a middle ground, compared to the previous historical occasions of 1972, 1978 or the year 2000.

For the first time, a constitutional making effort has taken some great pains through what termed as the Public Representation Committee (PRC) during January and May 2016 to gather the opinions of the people and their organizations at various levels on a multitude of constitutional issues that needs to be harmonized. Its Report is now published.[6] Whatever the weaknesses of this report or the Committee's inability to harmonize their own views, this effort is laudable. Be as it may, the report itself shows considerable imbalances prevailing on various questions and issues in constitution making. Therefore the task is marathon in harmonizing and balancing them. This is one reason why the constitution making process should be transparent and should not be confined to the Committee Rooms of the Parliament. There should be more open discussions on the media (printed, electronic and social) and there is a pressing need for weekly briefings by the Constituent Assembly spokespersons on the day to day progress. Most important is to win the 'trust of the people' and the outcome/s of the process should be people's friendly in its true sense. After all, unlike in the past occasions, the matter has to be finally decided by the people at a referendum.

This book is composed in three parts. Part I covers the 'general concerns on constitutional issues' ranging from 'why do we need a new constitution' to 'questions and answers on devolution,' and 'a suitable electoral system.' Part II consists of proposals made by the author to the Public Representation Committee (PRC) on Constitutional Reform running into twenty topics and a draft chapter on 'fundamental human rights and freedoms' and a proposed chapter on the 'local government system.' Part

---

[6] This report is available at www.yourconstitution.lk

III places the process of the new constitution making within a broader political perspective, analyzing the 'democratic political change in 2015' and emphasizing the importance of 'ethnic reconciliation' among other topics. The 'building of inter-ethnic social capital for reconciliation' is much emphasized. The Selected Bibliography at the end includes only the sources cited in the text, nevertheless gives a wide ranging theoretical and empirical studies relevant to the subject of new constitution making in Sri Lanka. It should be understood that while some of the articles are of popular/educational nature, the others are more of academic disposition. The substance in all of them, however, is based on independent research or observations without any partisan bias or personal/group interest.

ACKNOWLEDGMENTS

I take this opportunity to acknowledge and thank the consistent support and encouragement given by Emeritus Professor Graeme Gill, and Emeritus Professor Rodney Tiffen, at the Department of Government and International Relations, University of Sydney, for my academic work and publications. Same goes for Dr. S. I. Keethaponcalan, my former colleague, who is now the Chair of the Department of Conflict Resolution, Salisbury University, Maryland.

This publication was not possible without the support and enthusiasm of Nilantha Ilangamuwa, young Editor of the Sri Lanka Guardian, who kindly undertook formatting, designing of the cover page, and all organizational matters.

Thanks go to the Editor of the *Asian Tribune*, K. T. Rajasingham; Editor of the *Colombo Telegraph*, Uvindu Kurukulasuriya; and Editor of *The Island* daily newspaper, Prabath Sahabandu, apart from Nilantha of the *Sri Lanka Guardian*, who have published my articles including many of the present ones at various times. Much appreciation is equally to the Editor of the Tamil daily *Virakesari*, Veeragathy Thanabalasingham, who translated and published some of these articles. Equal appreciation is to Gamini Viyangoda for translating some of the articles into Sinhala and publishing in the *Ravaya* newspaper and *Yahapalanaya*. Thanks also due to various other websites for reproducing some of these articles.

I also wish to acknowledge with appreciation Dr. Asanga Welikala (University of Edinburgh) under whose editorship the present chapters 2 & 15 were initially published in *Reforming Sri Lankan Presidentialism* and *The Nineteenth Amendment to the Constitution* respectively (Centre for Policy Alternative publications).

This publication was inspired by the tireless work of two of my friends – Dr. Jayampathy Wickramaratne MP (President's Counsellor) and Lal Wijenayake (Attorney at Law) towards a new Constitution in Sri Lanka. Last but not least is my appreciation for the CreateSpace publishers and all staff of that great endeavor. Any error or omission however is my own responsibility and not of others.

ABBREVIATIONS

BOI – Board of Investment
CFA – Ceasefire Agreement
CP – Communist Party
CPA – Centre for Policy Alternatives
FPP – First Past the Post
ICCPR – International Covenant on Civil and Political Rights
ICESCR – International Covenant on Economic, Social and Cultural Rights
JO – Joint Opposition
JVP – Janatha Vimukthi Peramuna (People's Liberation Front)
LSSP – Lanka Sama Samaja Party (Lanka Equal Society Party)
LTTE – Liberation Tigers for Tamil Eelam
NMSJ - National Movement for Social Justice
NPC - National Peace Council
NSA – National State Assembly
OMP – Office of the Missing Persons
PR – Proportional Representation
PRC – Public Representation Committee
PTA - Prevention of Terrorisms Act
SLFP – Sri Lanka Freedom Party
TC – Tamil Congress
TNA – Tamil National Alliance
TULF – Tamil United Liberation Front
UNP – United National Party
UPFA – United People's Freedom Alliance

PART I

GENERAL CONCERNS OF CONSTITUTION MAKING

Laksiri Fernando

1

Democratic Dilemma in Sri Lanka

"Democracy cannot succeed unless those who express their choice are prepared to choose wisely." - Franklin D. Roosevelt

Since independence in 1948, Sri Lanka (then Ceylon) has experienced major shifts and changes in its political system quite extraordinary in the South Asian context in two main counts compared to India, Pakistan or Bangladesh. On the one hand, compared to India, the changes have been extremely volatile and far-reaching, placing the system almost at the brink of deviating from the accepted norms of democracy. Such major turning points have been 1972, 1978 and 2010. On the other hand, compared to Pakistan or Bangladesh, Sri Lanka has never plunged into military rule or dictatorship where the constitution was suspended, abrogated or completely by passed.[7] All the shifts and changes have so far been within the broad constitutional system.

In the past, Sri Lanka was prominent among democratic observers as a country which pioneered universal franchise in 1931 in Asia and preserved a system of 'liberal democracy' well into the early 1970s. Samuel P. Huntington classified 'Ceylon' as a country of the fourth period of democratic development however with mixed trends.[8] The pretensions

---

[7] See Ayesha Jalal, *Democracy and Authoritarianism in South Asia: A Comparative and Historical Perspective*, Harvard University Press, Massachusetts, 1995.

[8] Samuel P. Huntington, "Will More Countries Become Democratic?"

became rather blurred after 1972 and more so when a presidential system of government was installed instead of the traditional system of parliamentary government in 1978.[9]

In recent decades, Sri Lanka was more prominent and controversial because of its ethnic conflict and the separatist civil war. Human rights became the main focus of international concern. Many efforts at peaceful resolution of the conflict, national and international, did not bear fruit. In an extremely complex web of forces operating within and outside the country, Sri Lanka was at the edge of separation with the possibility of military rule both in the North and the South in a divided country. In an unexpected turn of events within a short span of time (2006-2009), however, the separatist forces were defeated, extremely under controversial circumstances, and overt stability became established with considerable cost to the democratic institutions and values.[10]

The Argument

There are many important research themes and problems that any investigator would encounter in studying the political system in Sri Lanka. This essay however focuses on one set of problems that the country has been confronting to do with its 'form and substance,' on the one hand, and the limitations of the 'horizontal spread' to capture and address the complexities of its multi-ethnic and diverse society on the other. While the first has a lot to do with human rights and the effectiveness of the civil society in the country, the second focuses more on the issues of decentralization, devolution, subsidiarity, and local governance. These are all about democratic imbalances, and to the author, they constitute one of the most important democratic dilemmas in Sri Lanka.

Democracy has been mainly a vertical phenomenon until recently without much horizontal spread except for formal local government institutions.[11]

Political Science Quarterly 99 (2), Summer 1984, p. 196.

[9] A. J. Wilson, *The Gaullist System in Asia: The Constitution of 1978*, Macmillan, London, 1980.

[10] "Report of the Secretary-General's Panel of Experts on Accountability in Sri Lanka," 31 March 2011. www.un.org/News/dh/infocus/Sri_Lanka/POE_Report_Full.pdf

[11] This study has not ventured into the theoretical arguments on 'vertical vs. horizontal democracy' although these exist. Important might an initial article by S. L. Hurley, "Rationality, Democracy and Leaky Boundaries: Vertical vs. Horizontal Modularity," *Journal of Political Philosophy* 7 (2), 1999,

The unitary constitution of the state was its main basis. The introduction of devolution has been belated (1987) thus with upheavals, and this has been a major reason for the eruption of ethnic conflict threatening the very survival of the democratic institutions. The vertical nature of democracy also was closely related to the other major imbalance between the 'form and substance' of democratic institutions. The institutional structure was authoritarian in nature and kept human rights and civil society activities under its yoke. Both imbalances are intrinsically interlinked and dialectically interconnected.

The main descriptive argument of this article is the following. At the beginning of democracy after independence (1948), the political system largely confined to the limited 'Westernized' elite and to them there was substance. The horizontal spread did not make much sense to them or was not necessary. However, when large masses came into the picture or democratic fold (1956), not only the substance but also the form eroded (1972 and 1978). There was also rupture within the vertical structures as a result of the ethnic conflict (1983). Consequently, horizontal democracy spread mainly in the form of the provincial council system under the Indian pressure (1987). There are new efforts to consolidate the vertical structures after the end of the war (2010) ostensibly to prevent new separatist movements. Irrespective of the above upheavals, the main democratic form and some significant substance have fortunately survived because of the traditions of franchise, people's participation, competitive multi-party system and international pressure. There are emerging middle classes in the rural Sri Lanka. The country may go through some further ruptures or regime changes (electorally) but the main trend at the next turn might be to look for more democracy and not less.[12]

Shifts and Changes

The best way to capture the major shifts and changes in the political system since independence and assess their impact on democratic form and substance is to make a comparison between the past (1948) and the present (2012). The purpose of the following Table 1 is to do so. Eleven characteristics are selected for this purpose and brief remarks are made assessing the changes.

---

pp. 126-146.

[12] This was a prediction in 2012 which became true in 2015.

Table 1
A Balance Sheet of Democracy, 1948-2012

Past (1948)	Present (2012)	Remarks
1. Unitary Constitution	1. Unitary Constitution with devolution	1. Partial progress with ambiguities
2. Head of State (British Monarchy) as nominal executive	2. Head of State (Republic) as Executive President	2. Recognition as republic. Erosion through concentration of power
3. Elected government headed by PM directly responsible to Parliament	3. Elected government headed by President indirectly responsible to Parliament	3. Considerable erosion of responsible government
4. Elected House of Representatives on first-past-the post	4. Elected Parliament on proportional representation (PR)	4. Representative character remains. PR creates instability and gap between voters and representatives
5. Second chamber to represent the unrepresented	5. No second chamber	5. Erosion of checks and balances
6. Independent judiciary without political influence	6. Ostensibly independent judiciary with political influence	6. Judiciary becoming controversial
7. Public Service independently appointed	7. Public Service with political interference	7. Erosion of impartiality of service delivery

8. Universal franchise and free and fair elections	8. Universal franchise extended, but free and fair elections occasionally compromised	8. Retention of basic norms with erosion of best practices
9. Multi and competitive party system	9. Party system retains with restrictions on independent candidates	9. Remains democratic. Restrictions controversial
10. Unhindered freedom of expression, press, assembly and organization	10. Restrictions remain irrespective of the end of war	10. Freedoms remain ambivalent
11. Peaceful and congenial political culture for democracy	11. Scars of violence still remains, political culture tending to condone authoritarianism	11. Stability established after 2009 with questions on nature of political culture

The following are further explanations. The first constitution (1947), promulgated one year before the formal independence, was a unitary constitution without any semblance of decentralization or devolution.[13] This continued to be the case in the succeeding two constitutions of 1972 and 1978 until devolution under the 13th Amendment was introduced in 1987 under India pressure. The devolution introduced can be considered the most progressive measure to expand horizontal democracy after independence and to reconcile the ethnic conflict although the situation after the war still prevails with ambiguities.

Sri Lanka achieved independence in 1948 under the British Monarchy. However, there was no common heritage between the two countries. Therefore, Sri Lanka moving away from the Monarchy and establishing a Republic in 1972 was a sign of political maturity. Initially thereafter, Head of State or the President was a nominal executive. It was in 1978 that the President became the Head of the Executive closely linking the state system into partisan politics. It was like 'one step forward two steps back.'

---

[13] Ivor Jennings, *The Constitution of Ceylon*, Oxford University Press, Bombay, 1953.

Sri Lanka was known as a cabinet system of government with collective responsibility to Parliament until 1977. However, when the system moved to a presidential system of government in 1978 this responsibility became blurred. Although in democratic theory, the presidential system is an accepted form of democratic government,[14] the introduction of the presidential system in Sri Lanka was justified by its architect as an executive system free from the 'whims and fancies of the elected Parliament.'[15] The change into the presidential system of government marked a major turning point in the country; moving away from a 'liberal democratic system.'

The second chamber was abolished in 1972. Earlier it functioned as a check on the House of Representatives and allowed the unrepresented sections to be represented in it including the minorities. When devolution was introduced in 1987, the absence of a second chamber constituted a major weakness. There was a considerable erosion of independence of the judiciary since 1972. The theory of 'people's sovereignty' and 'supremacy of Parliament' were the justifications for the deviation. Although the independence of the judiciary was accepted in theory, in practice there were constraints having the judiciary to depend on the executive.

There have been several changes to the way the public servants were appointed and managed. Since 1972, major appointments were done by Cabinet decisions. There were attempts to re-establish the independence and professionalism of several state services such as the judiciary, the public service and the police. The 17th Amendment to the Constitution was such an effort in October 2001 which became reversed in September 2010 under the 18th Amendment. There are considerable adverse implications on accountability, transparency and political impartiality as a result of the latter change.

Universal franchise and popular participation have remained major institutional pillars of the democratic architecture with deviations and reversals in certain junctures. In 1949, the Tamil plantation workers of Indian origin were disenfranchised with their exclusion from the citizenship.[16] It took more than four decades to re-award franchise to those

---

[14] David Beetham and Kevin Boyle, *Introducing Democracy*, UNESCO, Paris, 2009. p.61.

[15] President J. R. Jayewardene was the architect of the constitution. See *Selected Speeches, 1944-1973*, H. W. Cave, Colombo, 1974.

[16] S. U. Kodikara, *Indo-Ceylon Relations since Independence*. Ceylon Institute of World Affairs, Colombo, 1965.

who obtained Sri Lankan citizenship. In 1956, the age of franchise was reduced from 21 years to 18 years. Franchise and people's commitment to franchise remain a major strength of democracy with high voter turnout at elections, at times nearing 85 percent. The degree of political participation has also increased and not decreased. Equally important pillar of democracy has been the competitive and multi-party system, the conventional-liberal United National Party (UNP) and the socialist-nationalist Sri Lanka Freedom Party (SLFP) being the two main parties. There were 62 other political parties registered with the Elections Commissioner by February 2012.[17] Political parties initially emerged out of the nationalist movement at the beginning of the 20th century and remain strong even today.

Freedom of expression, press, assembly and association remained largely unhindered until the first insurrection in 1971. After that insurrection, Sri Lanka has experienced several erosions of all these freedoms particularly during the thirty years of war. Emergency regulations and the Prevention of Terrorisms Act (PTA) were the major instruments used in curtailing freedoms directly and indirectly. Even in recent periods, disappearances of journalists, killings and attacks on 'free media' institutions have taken place.

Political culture of the country was largely peaceful at the beginning of independence with only rare incidents of political violence. The situation changed dramatically in the 1970s, perhaps as a result of the population pressure and new generations of youth emerging with disillusionment and frustration.[18] The seats of education, not only universities but also high schools became volatile. The change of the political culture could well be attributed to the breakdown in education and deteriorating standards in particularly vernacular newspapers. The overall picture of the shifts and changes of the democratic system is mixed.

Vertical Dilemma

As it is shown by the above assessment, there is a clear dilemma of democracy which arises largely because of the vertical character of the system. To date the country remains mainly a vertical democracy irrespective of the introduction of devolution. The devolution has not taken many roots due to several reasons. Its origins are not completely indigenous; it did not work in the North-East during the war (1989-2009)

---

[17] Mahinda Deshapriya, Elections Commissioner, Circular dated 17 February 2012.

[18] Gamini Samaranayake, *Political Violence in Sri Lanka, 1971-1978*. Gyan Books, New Delhi, 2007.

where it was primarily meant; and vertical hierarchies at the center, both political and bureaucratic, always tend to resist devolution and even decentralization.

The vertical character of democracy is based on the following institutions and processes. There are 20.8 million people in Sri Lanka and around 14 million of them (or 67 percent) are registered voters after attaining the age of 18. Parliamentary elections are held every five years and presidential in six years while both could be conducted earlier if necessary. The initial single member (with few multimember) constituency system of elections akin to Britain is now changed for larger 22 electoral districts electing 196 members to Parliament consisting of 225 members, under proportional representation. Other than voting for a party, the voters have three preferential votes for the individual candidates of that party. The other 29 members of Parliament are appointed from a national list of parties according to the proportions of vote that the parties obtain at the national level. Here the leaders of parties have major discretion in selecting national list members. Independent candidates can contest but only 'as a group' unlike in the past. The provision undermines their true independence of those candidates. All decisions regarding elections are made by an Election Commissioner subject to appeal to the Supreme Court. Functions of the Election Commissioner are carried out independent from the incumbent government nevertheless under immense pressure at times.[19]

Many of the deviations from the accepted democratic norms occur during election campaigns where state apparatus, including public funds, are misused on behalf of the incumbent government. Otherwise, the existing election laws are formulated to ensure free and fair elections like in a liberal democratic country. It is not only the government that deviates from the election rules but also the opposition parties. Other weaknesses of the election processes arise at polling stations or counting centers with occasional violence, intimidation or harassment. Inaction or explicit bias on the part of the police is a major reason for the situation. The police in Sri Lanka are one of the main obstacles in the democratic setup.[20] Most of the violations are perpetrated by individual candidates or their supporters across the political spectrum. There is not only inter-party violence but also intra-party ones mainly due to the competition for preferential votes under

---

[19] Commonwealth Expert Team, "Report of Sri Lanka Presidential Election, 26 January 2010," Commonwealth Secretariat, 2010, p. 9.

[20] See Executive Summary, "Final Report on Election Related Violence and Malpractices, Parliamentary Election 2010," Centre for Monitoring Election Violence (CMEV), April 2010.

the PR system.

There is a dual process in electing governments, presidential and parliamentary, which routinely favors an incumbent government. For example, in January 2010, presidential election was held and the incumbent President was re-elected. Even during the election, the incumbent government continued with the President and a Prime Minister and a Cabinet of Ministers. Thereafter, in April 2010, elections for Parliament were held and the incumbent coalition was returned with a bigger majority. Even during the elections, although Parliament was dissolved, the Cabinet of Ministers continued to hold office. Thereafter, a new Prime Minister and a Cabinet of Ministers were appointed by the President. It is possible to argue that the procedure has some obvious electoral advantages to an incumbent government against an opposition. While this may be true, there are examples of governmental change through the election process without extra parliamentary means in recent times.

In 1994, there was a major change of government after electing a new President from a different party. Again there was a change of government in 2001 when people elected a different party in Parliament to that of the President and the President had to act almost as a nominal executive. Although not from a different party, a new President was elected in 2005 with completely a different policy. A change of government is possible through the election process. But what has become important is not parliamentary election but presidential election. As many parties are represented in Parliament and political crossovers are common, it has become easy for a President to manage or manipulate parliamentary majorities. This is not healthy for democracy. The other defect is the lack of by elections to Parliament to reflect the changing party preferences of the people as a warning signal to any incumbent government. The local government elections are not effective in this respect as they largely depend on the central government and tend to return those who support the incumbent government.[21]

However, a change could happen through the provincial councils in between or closer to parliamentary or presidential elections. Crossovers are common even in provincial councils but what might be decisive are changes at elections. Prior to the election as President in 1994, Chandrika Kumaratunga became the Chief Minister of the Southern Provincial Council in 1993 through provincial council elections. The Western

---

[21] At elections held in March 2011 for 234 local government institutions, the ruling UPFA took control of 205 local bodies.

Provincial Council also went to the opposition signaling an impending major change in politics. Therefore, given a very strict structure of vertical democracy where avenues are almost closed for changes within a given tenure of office of a President at the center, the horizontal democracy through the second tier of governance or provincial councils supply some avenues of political change.

There are many other defects of this vertical democracy. The political process is mainly one way traffic upwards, people basically electing governments with long intervals but without much mechanism or processes for the governments or people's representatives to fulfil their accountability to the people. There is no possibility of changing the governments or representatives in between elections. Hardly there are possibilities of influencing them. This is why the freedom of expression, the media and association, particularly to mean the civil society activities, are important. Another connected problem is the weakening of the 'checks and balances' throughout years since independence. There were many mechanisms of checks and balances initially in the 1947 Constitution. The existence of a second chamber, independence of the judiciary with judicial review, independence and invisibility of the public service and the possibility of changing a government through a no confidence motion were some of them. They all have changed now to a larger degree. Although a successful no confidence motion is still a possibility, there is no practical possibility of an impeachment motion against a President.[22] A successful no confidence motion against a government might or might not lead to a change of government as the matter finally rests with the discretion of the President.

It is important to note that Sri Lanka's curtailment of checks and balances in the constitutional system has been largely ideological. It came through a mixture of nationalism and socialism with also certain principles drawing from British utilitarianism. The initial constitutional changes were made in the 1972 Constitution enshrining the concept of the supremacy of parliament as an embodiment of people's sovereignty. It proclaimed that the newly created National State Assembly (NSA) is the main depositary of legislative, executive and judicial power of the people although they would be implemented through different arms. It was a milder version of people's power which disregarded basic notions of constitutionalism. Although the previous constitution also was a unitary constitution, for the first time, the 1972 Constitution declared Sri Lanka as a sovereign and unitary republic. Under the unitary concept of the state, federalism or devolution was

---

[22] N. M. Perera, *Critical Analysis of the New Constitution of the Sri Lankan Government,* V. S. Raja, Colombo, 1979.

rejected. All vertical aspects of the political system were strengthened. This continued even after the 1978 Constitution until the 13th Amendment in 1987 that introduced a certain degree of horizontal democracy or devolution.

There can be a political economy or class interpretation for the changes that have taken place within the vertical democratic system in Sri Lanka. When the urban elite or the bourgeoisie supported by the urban middle classes initially prevailed in the political system (1948 to 1956), liberal or constitutional democracy prevailed. When the rural elite or the rural bourgeoisie supported by the rural masses started to influence through new political formations, the democratic system deviated to incorporate populism and 'popular democracy' (1970-1977). This appeared as an alternative to liberal democracy.

Tensions in a Plural Society

Vertical democracy always stood uneasy on top of Sri Lanka's plural society. This has always been a major contradiction. There are three main aspects to the plural nature of the society: ethnic, religious and political. One may add urban-rural dichotomy into it. However, this essay gives emphasis on ethnic and religious plurality.

The following Tables 2 represents the main ethnic and religious groups in society for two census years of 1946 and 1981. In 1991 no census was conducted and in 2001 the census was limited to 18 districts out of 25; all due to the war situation in the country since 1983. The data of the 2012 census is not yet available.

Table 2
Ethnic and Religious Groups in Sri Lanka

Category	1946	1981
Ethnicity		
Sinhalese	69.41	73.95
North-east Tamils	11.02	12.71
Hill Country Tamils	11.73	5.51
Moors	5.61	7.05
Others	2.24	0.77
Religion		
Buddhist	64.51	69.30
Hindu	19.83	15.48
Muslim	6.56	7.56
Christian	7.62	7.62
Other	0.06	0.06

Source: Census and Statistics

As the figures show, Sri Lanka is a multi-ethnic and multi-religious society with significant four ethnic communities and four similar religious groups. Two years before independence, in 1946, the majority Sinhalese comprised around 70 per cent of the population which rose to nearly 74 percent by 1981. The proportional increase was mainly due to the repatriation of a significant number of Tamil plantation workers of Indian origin back to India after two agreements in 1964 and 1974 with the Indian government. As a result, the percentage of Hill Country Tamils decreased from nearly 12 percent to less than 6 percent during the same period. Although the other ethnic groups such as the North-East Tamils and the Muslims also gained a proportional increases (see Table), those were not significant compared to the edge that the majority Sinhalese gained due to the repatriation measures. It is possible that the proportional strengths of the two main groups, the Sinhalese and the Tamils, have further widened by now. Nearly one million Tamils is supposed to have left the country as Diaspora after 1983 communal violence against them.[23] An unknown number on both sides, perhaps over 100,000, has also been killed and more on the Tamil side during the war.

Compared to other countries in the Indian sub-continent or Asia, the ethnic composition in Sri Lanka is less complicated with only four main groups, but perhaps that is a reason for the sharp political polarization between them. Under the previously analyzed vertical democratic structure, there is a possibility that the majority Sinhalese could govern the country without compromising with the minorities. That is also the way that democracy is understood or rather misunderstood in Sri Lanka by a great majority of the ordinary people.[24] It is believed that minority Tamils and Muslims should respect the decisions of the majority Sinhalese. This is where the democratic education has been a major failure in the country. During 1948 and 1956, there was some form of power sharing between different ethnic groups, the main Tamil party of that time - the Tamil Congress (TC) - participating in the Cabinet. However, there was no power sharing between 1956 and 1965. Although power sharing arrangements were resurrected during 1965-70, it became also strongly resisted by the emerging Tamil youth movements and militancy.[25]

Apart from ethnic factors in a multi-cultural society, language and religious factors are important. Among the two main competing ethnic groups – the Sinhalese and Tamils - there is a clear language demarcation. Both of these ethnic groups are identified mainly in terms of language and partly by religion. A major reason for irritation and friction between them is the difficulty in understanding each other's language. When the government in 1956 made the Sinhalese the sole official language, it was a direct rejection of the Tamil identity in the country. To demonstrate the significance of the language issue, a left leader during the debate on the official language bill in 1956 stated "one language two countries, two languages one country." The language issue is still a continuing sore point although formally now Tamil is 'also recognized as an official language.'[26]

---

[23] International Crisis Group, "The Sri Lankan Tamil Diaspora after the LTTE," Asia Report 186, February 2010.

[24] Ruki Fernando, "Key challenges of democratization in post war and post-election in Sri Lanka," (monograph) Law and Society Trust, May 2010.

[25] Ambalavanar Siverajah, *Politics of Tamil Nationalism in Sri Lanka*, South Asian Books, New Delhi, 1996.

[26] It is important note that when Tamil was recognized as an official language in the 13th Amendment in 1987, the revision exactly said "Tamil is also an official language." The wording itself was discriminatory.

As the above table shows, religion is also important in multi-cultural demarcations. While the majority of the Sinhalese are Buddhists, the majority of the Tamils are Hindus. Although popular Buddhism incorporates many of the Hindu rituals and practices, at the level of the religious hierarchy, the two religions are strictly kept apart. Another important minority group in society is the Moors or the Muslims. They are mostly identified by the religion and consist around 7 percent of the population. Although the Moors or Muslims do not have their own language, their religion is strong enough to give them a cohesive identity. As the Muslims are demographically dispersed in many small areas, they are mostly keen in strong local government institutions rather than large provincial councils. Another distinct group is the Christians, both of Catholics and Protestants. There has been a decrease of their proportion between 1946 and 1981 from 9.06 percent to 7.62 percent. Two reasons for the decline are their conversion to Buddhism or Hinduism through intermarriages and their migration to the countries like Australia, Canada or Britain. A major frustration among this group is the special status given to Buddhism in the Constitutions of 1972 and 1978 contrary to what is expected as religious tolerance and equality. The Christians are the only group who cut across the ethnic divide between the Sinhalese and the Tamils.

There is a clear lack of understanding of pluralism, multiculturalism and minority rights in Sri Lanka.[27] The other side of the same coin is the apparent extremism in agitating for minority rights. It is possible that different groups led or misled by partisan politics were fighting for a small pie. Prior to 1977, Sri Lanka was mainly a stagnant economy with welfare and 'stratified equity.' The Sinhalese or at least their elite got the 'lions share' and the Tamils used to get some share under a controlled and a closed economy. With the open economy after 1977, the economy started to change and the pie started to expand. The conflict apparently intensified. The 1983 communal riots were explained in this kind of political economy perspective.[28] Prior to that there were a series of small riots beginning in 1977 aftermath of the elections in that year. However, the economic factors are not clear determinants of the ethnic conflict or any other issue of the

---

[27] See Neil DeVotta, *Blowback: Linguistic Nationalism, Institutional Decay and Ethnic Conflict in Sri Lanka*, Stanford University Press, Stanford, 2004.

[28] Newton Gunasinghe, "The Open Economy and Its Impact on Ethnic Relations in Sri Lanka." In Deborah Winslow and Michael D. Woost, *Economy, Culture and Civil War in Sri Lanka*, Indiana University Press, Bloomington, 2004, pp. 99-114.

democratic dilemma. They only pinpoint to some of the underlying forces that we are concerned about. What particularly lacking were the intermediary factors or forces such as the civil society organizations and proper understanding of human rights.

Imbalance in Human Rights

No democracy is successful without a vibrant civil society, based on strong citizenry. It is the depositary of civil rights and the preserve of many other rights in the economic, social, cultural and political spheres. All the defects of human rights, however, cannot be attributed to the weaknesses of a civil society. The primary responsibility undoubtedly goes to the State and the political parties. Individual freedoms are preserved, whether it is of an ordinary citizen, a voter, a journalist, a writer or an academic, to the extent that the State keeps away or more correctly the State is kept away from society as much as possible without interference. The civil society should be vigilant. However, there are other rights that the State should directly deliver under certain circumstances, especially in developing countries like Sri Lanka. This is where that a contradiction might arise between the deliverance of rights in the economic and social sphere by the State and the preservation of other rights in the civil and political sphere. While Sri Lanka is a major example of this contradiction, certain weaknesses of the civil society underpin this situation emerging out of largely an underdeveloped political economy.

The curtailment of civil or political rights cannot be justified in order to deliver economic and social rights. This is only an argument. It is the advantages that accrue to the State in delivering economic and social rights that allows the opportunities for the State to keep the civil and political rights at bay. The neglect of rights is somewhat inherent to any type of State, unless it is tamed and constrained by rules and regulations through constitution and institutions in a democratic fashion. An example is appropriate to explain this dilemma. Sri Lanka is a country where social welfare or social protection is high. Apart from the services in the spheres of health and education, a direct poverty alleviation program is being implemented since 1995 which is called *Samurdhi* meaning 'prosperity' assistance. Before that, a similar program called *Janasaviya* was in operation. Under *Samurdhi*, direct monetary benefits are given to the recipients and in April 2012 the number of families who received the benefits was counted as over 1.6 million.[29] This is around 35 percent of all families in the country

---

[29] Basil Rajapaksa, Minister of Economic Development, *Daily Financial Times*, 12 April 2012.

and all could not be necessarily considered below the poverty line. While there are recognized poverty alleviation outcomes of the program, it is also considered one of the main political bases of the current political regime in Sri Lanka. It is strongly alleged that not only the recipients but also those who are appointed to conduct the program, around 27,000 *Samurdhi* officers, are being used not only to create a support base but also to coerce and control the political opponents particularly in the villages.

Human rights in Sri Lanka are undoubtedly a complex jumble. The belated arrival of the notions of international human rights is one reason. Although traditional Buddhist or Hindu teachings have much respect for human dignity, the notions are not practical enough to safeguard the requirements of modern human rights in a complex society such as today. There was no bill of rights in the first independent constitution except certain safeguards on minority rights in the sphere of legislation. Even they were not good enough to prevent discriminatory legislation on citizenship (1948), franchise (1949) or language (1956). The first constitution which had a chapter on fundamental rights was the 1972 Constitution. Yet the rights promulgated in the constitution were not justiciable. Thereafter, when the 1978 Constitution incorporated a justiciable fundamental rights chapter in its text, the practical situation of human rights had deteriorated to a great extent that mere legislation or judicial processes were not sufficient.[30] Sri Lanka could join the UN only in 1955. Although thereafter, the country's ratification rate of international human rights instruments can be considered fairly high, a commensurate practice has not accompanied to promote and protect human rights in a tangible manner.

Two institutional mechanisms that are in place to protect fundamental rights or human rights in general are the Supreme Court and the Human Rights Commission. They in fact encounter considerable pressures or obstacles in performing their tasks emerging particularly from political authorities and the police. Especially under the circumstances of conflict, insurrection or war that the country has been undergoing for a long period, the safeguarding of human rights has been a surmountable task. It was extremely difficult to keep a track on violations, to trace the violators and to take remedial or punitive measures as incidence and violations have been rapidly accumulating. Many of the violations were linked to the breakdown of law and order.

There are three major observations that can be made in general terms in

---

[30] See for more details Jayampathy Wickramaratne, *Fundamental Rights in Sri Lanka*, Navrang, New Delhi, 1996.

respect of human rights in Sri Lanka. First is the fact that the country is considerably poor in the recognition of cultural rights or the rights of minorities. The recognition of these rights may require a considerable change in the political culture and legal reforms to make the internationally accepted principles operational. Second is the fact that Sri Lanka's record in terms of the implementation of economic and social rights is comparatively commendable except that the deliverance of these rights is at times politically abused. The third is the fact that the implementation or prevalence of civil and political rights has fluctuated from time to time considerably, depending on the political circumstances.

Devolution and Horizontal Spread

Vertical democracy by nature was so hierarchical, often resisted to spread its institutions throughout the country since independence. It was largely a legacy of the colonial rule. The British authorities preferred centralized institutions for convenience or to prevent rebellion and resistance. Only at the latter stages of the colonial administration that local government institutions were introduced, yet with limited powers and functions.[31]

The present devolution has come about as a result of the Indian pressure in 1987 since the conflict in Sri Lanka was a major internal political issue, overflowing into Tamil Nadu.[32] After an agreement between the two countries - the Indo-Lanka Accord - the Constitution was amended to constitute the present Provincial Councils with a Finance Commission to recommend and oversee the funding for them. The model followed was basically Indian. Under the 13th Amendment and the Provincial Councils Act, the Provincial Councils are elected every five years as a second tier of governance with a mandate for wide ranging functions and powers.[33] All in all, 37 functions including several revenue and tax powers are attributed in what is called the Provincial Council List. Likewise there is a Reserved List for the central government. Most controversial or ambiguous is the Concurrent List under which the central government could easily encroach into the matters of the Provincial Councils. Whatever the weaknesses of the present arrangements, which may be necessary to rectify fairly soon, the

---

[31] G. R. T. Leitan, *Local Government and Decentralized Administration in Sri Lanka*, Lake House, Colombo, 1979.

[33] Ranjith Amerasinghe et al (Ed.), *Twenty Years of Devolution: An Evaluation of the Working of Provincial Councils in Sri Lanka*, Institute for Constitutional Studies, Colombo, 2011.

provincial council system is the most progressive structural change that the democratic system in Sri Lanka has achieved since independence.

Devolution of power or the horizontal spread of democracy could be considered important mainly for three reasons: (1) for ethnic reconciliation by allowing the minority communities particularly the Tamils and/or Muslims to run their own councils (2) for economic development by ensuring balanced provincial development through the initiatives of provincial representatives and people and (3) for furtherance of democracy by allowing provincial dissent and ensuring opportunities for the opposition parties to run their own administration if the people so desire.

Although some political parties in the South initially were in opposition to the formation of Provincial Councils, subsequently almost all the parties have taken part in the provincial council elections and even taken up ministerial positions. Devolution or horizontal democracy seems to have a natural normative appeal to the people. Obviously more enthusiasm for the Provincial Councils has come from the parties in the North and the East. The non-operation of Provincial Councils in the North and the East since 1990 due to ongoing war undoubtedly was a setback for the spread of horizontal democracy. In 2008, however, the elections for the East were held and the Council is now constituted. The elections for the Northern Provincial Council still to be held and in fact overdue. It is difficult to say how far the spread of democracy with an active civil society, understanding of human rights, initiatives for ethnic reconciliation has taken place as a result of the institution of the Provincial Councils yet. This is a matter for further research. However, it is clear that as a result of the Provincial Councils a new layer of political leaders at the provincial level has emerged. Another positive feature is that the local government system is now functioning under the Provincial Councils; and not under the central government. It is a convincing argument that both the accountability and the responsiveness of government are maximized when decision-makers are in close proximity to their citizens. This is the essence of subsidiarity.

Conclusion

Even if there is correlation or causality, between economic development and democracy, yet it is difficult to say at what level of economic development that societies embrace democracy partially or in full. This is where a political economy approach is necessary in broader terms in assessing the prospects for democracy. Sri Lanka, like India, embraced democracy at considerably a low level of economic development and managed to sustain a formal democratic system with regular elections and also changes of government for a long period of time. The secret perhaps was the strength of the political institutions that were in place at the time of independence and the commitment of at least good number of political parties and people for democracy. These could be considered fairly high in Sri Lanka. Nevertheless, as our analysis regarding the institutional 'shifts and changes' has shown, undoubtedly there have been deviations and aberrations and at times the system was at the brink of even collapse. It was our observation that Sri Lanka has entered into a critical stage with these changes that are more towards negative than positive. The imbalance between 'form and substance' has been substantial.

The horizontal spread of democracy has been low and late in Sri Lanka compared to India and the vertical structures were the most dominant, the Presidential System at the helm in the institutional edifice at times almost coalescing with authoritarianism. There were symptoms of this tendency in the past and there are strong symptoms also at present. The devolution or Provincial Council system introduced in 1987 could be considered the most welcome development in the country since independence, giving some room for the horizontal spread of democracy, although the system has not yet taken much root. The acid test of democracy in the coming future will be whether this system would be extended or abolished; or modified to make it more effective or ineffective.

Laksiri Fernando

2
Human Rights and the 1978 Constitution

"To deny people their human rights is to challenge their very humanity." - Nelson Mandela

If one takes 1978 as a landmark in dividing the post-independence history in Sri Lanka into two periods, three decades before (1948-1978) and three decades after (1978-2008), the latter may mark as satisfactory in human rights legal codification, the fundamental rights chapter in the 1978 Constitution as the forerunner, but abysmally horrendous in human rights violations in almost all spheres of national and international importance. The former was far better and salubrious, in comparison, although there was very little in terms of human rights codification. This irony indicates the importance of multitude of other socio-political factors as well as the overall constitutional conditions that affect a human rights situation in a country other than or irrespective of a fundamental rights chapter and other legal codifications which is the main message of this chapter. The overall constitutional conditions may mean the nature of the governmental system and whether the system is parliamentary or presidential to be more precise, other than the operation of the democratic rule of law in general.

Karel Vasak argued that *de jure* state is the first requirement for human rights to become a legal reality.[34] By legal reality, he didn't mean the mere existence of human rights in written law, but its actual legal practice through the whole gamut of rule of law. He explained that "Without

---

[34] K. Vasak (1982), "Human Rights: As a Legal Reality" In K. Vasak (ed.), *The International Dimensions of Human Rights* (Paris: UNESCO).

entering into theoretical discussions, it may simply be said that a *de jure* State is one in which all the authorities and all individuals are bound by pre-established general and impersonal rules, in a word, by *law*." It may only be added that 'rule of law' should be 'democratic rule of law' as Filip Spagnoli has emphasized.[35]

There can be many arguments against the 1978 Constitution that created conditions to the detriment of the human rights situation in the country that was already fragile due to similar or other reasons.[36] But the 1978 Constitution can be unreservedly marked as a turning point in constitutionally diluting the democratic rule of law by instituting Presidential powers that cannot be challenged in courts of law.[37] With impunity for the President, or under his/her direct authority, 'all authorities' could not be considered as 'bound by the pre-established general and impersonal rules' that Vasak talked about. What started as seemingly a benign growth in 1978 increasingly spread as a malignant tumor and today constitutes one of the dangerous cancers in the body politic. That is primarily the breakdown of democratic rule of law.

Based on Karel Vasak and other sources, and primarily based on empirical evidence of the human rights trajectory since 1978, this chapter argues that there has been an inevitable dichotomy between human rights and the 1978 Constitution which is one of the most authoritarian forms of presidential systems. As Vasak said:

Although in our time the law is hardly the expression of the general will, as Rousseau contended, it remains the most effective practical means for citizens to preserve the sphere of human rights from the executive, through the role which they play in choosing their legislative body. In other words, the law, insofar as it is the work of a parliament elected by the citizens, constitutes the sole possible legal basis for human rights. It is for this reason that human rights are bound to be more likely to exist in countries with parliamentary tradition.[38]

---

[35] Filip Spagnoli (2003), *Homo Democraticus: On the Universal Desirability and the Not So Universal Possibility of Democracy and Human Rights* (Buckinghamshire: Cambridge Scholars Press), p. 117.

[36] Among these reasons was the 1972 Constitution which clearly diluted the independence of the judiciary among other infringements.

[37] Article 35 (1) governed the impunity of the President. More than its legality, the impression became created that the President is virtually above the law.

[38] Vasak, op. cit. p. 6. Vasak implicitly of the view that human rights are more vulnerable under presidential systems than parliamentary democracies while also highlighting the importance of what he called 'political, economic and social

Political Background

The parliamentary general election in 1977 was already delayed by two years, the election that paved the way for the 1978 Constitution, which in itself signified a major aberration in the democratic system. The previous United Front (UF) government had already taken the advantage of the new constitution that they promulgated in 1972 to extend the tenure of the Parliament. Otherwise the election should have been held in 1975 and not in 1977, under the 1947 Constitution which fairly supplied a framework for the country's democratic system and human rights to function for nearly two and a half decades. The opposition led by the UNP also did not oppose the extension strong enough as if there was an implicit agreement between the two major parties, the SLFP and the UNP, to manipulate the democratic system in order that they acquire and remain in power alternatively.

The ruthless suppression of the 1971 youth insurrection was in the background and the youth unrest in the North was on the ascendancy with emergency laws being used for its suppression almost continuously until the election time. The traditional left, the LSSP and the CP, and the trade union movement had become virtually impotent by that time as a viable democratic opposition to the two major parties by being accessories to the UF and the 1972 Constitution. From the beginning of the democratic system in Sri Lanka, if the introduction of the universal franchise in 1931 could be taken as the main landmark, the left and the trade union movement played a decisive role in safeguarding democracy and people's rights, but in the 1970s this was not the case any longer.

The election and election results in 1977 also had a direct bearing on human rights. It was the last general election held under the first-past-the post (FPP) system. In the election results, what could be seen is a major imbalance created in the competitive party system. The UNP received 50.92 per cent of total votes polled and 140 seats in the 168 member parliament, gaining a 5/6 majority, while the previous ruling party, the SLFP, being reduced to 8 seats irrespective of receiving 29.72 per cent of the votes polled. Apart from the FPP system, sharp de-legitimization process of the previous government due to unpopular and anti-rights policies were

---

democracy' for the human rights preservation. In a more critical study on the subject, Matthew S. Shugart and John M. Carey (1992), *Presidents and Assemblies* (Cambridge: Cambridge University Press) offered the same conclusion but in a more analytical manner.

responsible for this major shift. The SLFP failed to become the alternative government or the official opposition in Parliament and the leader of the opposition was selected from the TULF, winning 18 seats but only 6.75 per cent of votes. The TULF was not aiming at an alternative government but a separate state or self-autonomy to the regions that they represented as declared in 1976.[39]

The 1977 election was a classic example of a hegemonic political party (UNP) ingeniously utilizing the people's unarticulated grievances on human rights issues to come into power but not fulfilling the underlying aspirations as these aspirations themselves are not firmly held by the civil society due to multitude of reasons. By this time, the notions of human rights were quite new to Sri Lanka except the rights advocated by the labor or the minorities. The rights of the labor or the minorities, on the other hand, were formulated in terms of left wing or other ideologies (i.e. nationalism) and not so much on the basis of universal human rights. The first human rights organization, the Civil Rights Movement (CRM), was formed in 1971 aftermath of the youth insurrection, first as purely a humanitarian organization. Most of the civil society organizations by this time were of welfare or religious nature. If intelligentsia could be considered as a major or necessary catalyst for human rights, they have not yet been attracted by this new philosophy of human rights on a professional basis.[40]

Sri Lanka saw major postelection violence in July-August 1977 with considerable death, casualties and property destruction. During the elections, the UNP leader declared that he would give 'one week holiday for the police in order that the people could celebrate the victory' to mean that the winning party could take revenge against the defeated.[41] Obviously, the UF supporters had taken revenge from their UNP opponents when they were in power (1970-77). Ironically the leftist supporters of the UF were the major casualties in the initial days facing arson attacks which spread against the Tamils in the hill country for not so obvious reasons. What was

---

[39] See Vaddukodai Resolution, 1976. S. I. Keethaponcalan (2009), *Conflict and Peace in Sri Lanka: Major Documents* (Colombo: Kumaran Book House), pp. 38-45.

[40] One exception, however, was the request of the Ceylon Rationalist Association (CRA) to incorporate fundamental rights as laid down in the Declaration of Human Rights of the United Nations in the proposed constitution of 1972 in a Memorandum sent to the Minister of Constitutional Affairs in September 1970. *Ground Views*, 14 June 2013.

[41] UTHR (J), "July 1983: Planned by the State or Spontaneous Mob Action?" http://www.uthr.org/Book/CHA11.htm Also see for electoral violence Sisira Pinnawala (2004), "Damming the Flood of Violence and Shoring Up of Civil Society," in S. H. Hasbullah and Barrie M. Morrison (ed.), *Sri Lankan Society in an Era of Globalization* (London: Sage Publications), p. 262.

underneath was the Sinhalese resentment that the main Tamil organization, the TULF, was asking for a separate state and had won 18 seats becoming the main opposition party in Parliament. The riots also commenced in Jaffna when the police started clashing with the civilians on 21 August triggered by a carnival incident. During the spate of violence throughout the country, 300 were killed mainly Tamils and over 1,000 became injured with homeless over 4,000.[42]

Most tragic was what the new Prime Minister, J. R. Jayewardene, who became the President later, told in Parliament on 18 August 1977 in response to what was happening particularly in the Jaffna Peninsula: "If you [Tamils] want to fight, let there be fight. If it is peace, let there be peace." [43] He added that "It is not what I am saying. The people of Sri Lanka will say that."

Philosophy Behind 1978

There was some idealism behind the 1972 Constitution, but in contrast, the 1978 Constitution was more pragmatic or crafty. The idealism of the 1972 was drawn from a mixture of tradition, socialism, nationalism and utilitarian constitutionalism. While the 1978 Constitution incorporating most of these aspects for convenience, turned the main governing structure upside down placing it on its head. If "what the 1972 Constitution did was to strengthen the legislature," as Nihal Jayawickrama has asserted,[44] the 1978 Constitution strengthened the Executive; and that was a new type of an Executive.

To understand this 'constitutional coup,' rendering constitutional idealism to the backburner within six years, one needs to focus on the historic speech made by its creator J. R. Jayewardene on 14 December 1966 before the Ceylon Association for the Advancement of Sciences (CAAS) proposing a presidential system of government for the first time.[45] The title

---

[42] Robert Kearney (1985), "Ethnic Conflict and the Tamil Separatist Movement in Sri Lanka," *Asian Survey*, 25 (9).

[43] Quoted by Donald L. Horowitz (2001), *The Deadly Ethnic Riot* (Berkeley: University of California Press), p. 91. Jayewardene was paraphrasing the Kandyan King Vimaladharmasuriya against the Dutch in early 17th century.

[44] Nihal Jayawickrama, "The Philosophy and Legitimacy of Sri Lanka's Republican Constitution," Keynote Address, Dr Colvin R de Silva Lecture, Ministry of Constitutional Affairs, 1 March 2008. http://www.sangam.org/2008/03/Republican_Constitution.php

[45] J. R. Jayewardene [2000], *Selected Speeches of Hon J. R. Jayewardene, 1944-1973* (Colombo: Jayewardene Centre), pp. 89-93. This speech was delivered a few days after a major pruning of a welfare measure (rice ration cut). Jayewardene was the

of his speech was "Science and Politics," if that were any indication of the approach. He said that "I am advocating a scientific approach to the study of some of our political questions." "Though there are different spheres of scientific study, science has a common method and approach to the subjects under its review. The scientific approach always seeks to gain and verify knowledge by exact observation and correct thinking," he further elaborated.

What were his exact observations and thinking? The main observation was in relation to Ceylon's failure to achieve economic progress or more precisely economic growth. "When we look back in retrospect over these 18 years [since independence in 1948] we find a record of achievement in some and failure in others," he noted. Then he said, "Yet the rate of growth of our population exceeds the rate of growth of our material resources so that, in very broad terms, the per capita wealth of our people has not kept pace with similar progress among the peoples of the developed nations of the world." There is no question that his observation was by and large correct but not necessarily his prescribed solution. There are many interpretations as to why Sri Lanka failed in its economic progress compared to, for example, Singapore or Malaysia, and there was a failure on his part to look at the conditions necessary for economic progress as a comprehensive package.[46] Instead, he was looking at or exaggerating some of the weaknesses in the democratic structure mainly based on his own liking as a conservative and authoritarian politician and this particular thinking had many adverse future consequences on the human rights situation in Sri Lanka.

J. R. Jayewardene had clear misgivings about popular democracy in the country. He said "It is argued that the politicians in power know what is wrong in the economy, they are aware of the remedy, but the desire to be popular and to secure a majority of votes at a general election prevents them taking the correct remedial measures." He added that "It should, however, be remembered that among the emerging nations in the continents of Africa and Asia, only two countries, India and Ceylon, have preserved the democratic system of Government intact…" He said the following, questioning the relevance of human rights in terms of 'human satisfaction.'

Minister of State in an uneasy cabinet of four parties. All quotations in this section are from that speech.

[46] In the same year a prominent economist perceived the country's economic problems in a more structural context. Donald R. Sondgrass (1966), *Ceylon: An Export Economy in Transition* (Homewood: R. D. Irwin).

A democratic system of Government includes what are termed democratic freedoms, the freedom to vote, freedom of opposition, freedom of speech and writing, and the rule of law, among other freedoms. Do these freedoms alone satisfy the people? I do not think so.

His question and answer were most important: 'Do these freedoms alone satisfy the people?' He very clearly stated that 'he didn't think so.' The answer could mean, under a different context, that he was emphasizing the economic and social rights instead of purely civil and political rights. But that was not completely the case.[47] Apart from his emphasis on 'per capita wealth' he did talk about "the failure to provide material comforts" in which he included "lower cost of living, employment, housing facilities and adequate leisure." However, his road map for achieving them was rigmarole and doubtful. Instead of ensuring those rights to the people, he was advocating a restricted democratic system where in the long run those 'material comforts' might be achieved but not necessarily on an equitable basis. What he emphasized was economic growth on the basis of pure or unfettered 'free economy, private enterprise and profit making.'[48]

As a senior politician, he was however careful not to reject democratic freedoms altogether. He summarized to say, "While counting the preservation of democratic freedoms as one of our achievements since Independence, we have not achieved the economic freedom that our people are entitled to. This has been our major failure." The following was his blue print for constitutional reform.

If then the democratic government has failed in some aspects, we should not hesitate to think of changes and amendments in that system where necessary. Parliament intends to examine the whole system of democratic government in our country, and while maintaining the basic freedoms of democracy, which in my opinion have not failed and need no change, adopt such reforms as would help the nation to solve its problems effectively and expeditiously. (My emphasis).

---

[47] The controversy over the primacy of economic/social rights vs. civil/political rights was very much alive during this time. However, Henry Shue (1980), *Basic Rights: Subsistence, Affluence and U.S. Foreign Policy* (Princeton: Princeton University Press) disputed the strict dichotomy and Amartya Sen (1999), *Development as Freedom* (Oxford: Oxford University Press) offered a new dimension to the understanding.

[48] A major casualty when this policy was applied in 1977 was the trade union movement. Laksiri Fernando (1988), "The Challenge of the Open Economy: Trade Unionism in Sri Lanka" in Roger Southall (ed.), *Trade Unions and New Industrialization of the Third World* (London: Zed Press).

This was the first time that a national leader proposed to dilute the democratic system in the country. The reason given was the 'failure of democratic government,' and as he said, 'in some aspects.' He wanted to maintain only the 'basic freedoms of democracy' but not all. Even that was quite reluctantly, as it is clear from the language that he used. The dilution of democracy, in his opinion, "would help the nation to solve its problems effectively and expeditiously."

Jayewardene proposed more precisely two major changes that became the cornerstones of the 1978 Constitution. First was the dilution of the representative system through an ambiguous PR system and the second was the introduction of an executive presidential system instead of the prevailing parliamentary system, both with considerable repercussions on the human rights situation in the country. On the issue of representation he first said, "Universal franchise and free exercise of the vote are necessary prerequisites of democracy" and then added "however." He was not happy that the electors elect their representatives directly. He instead wanted the voters to vote for a party and then the party decides whom to select from a list. "The electoral system which prevails here today, where the electors elect his legislator according to defined electoral areas, is not necessarily the best for our country," he said. Then he focused on a different system saying, "In some democratic countries political parties put forward a list of names of candidates seeking election; the legislators are then chosen from this list, the number depending on the votes cast for each party."

As it was correctly understood those days, his proposal was a 'list system' and proportional representation was only an appendage or an icing to the cake. He wanted to abolish the 'electorates' and that abolition eventually spelled disaster to the democratic system that the people were accustomed to since 1931. More precisely, he wanted to unplug the legislators from the voter base saying "There are no electorates. The voter votes for the Party and not for a particular candidate." He did have a particular logic or a concern when he said, "Today's electoral system in our country precludes the best equipped men and women from taking part in our political life." However, the proposed 'solution' was worse than the existing problem. The introduced PR system under the 1978 Constitution, with preferential voting for party candidates on the district basis, in fact produced a breed of legislators who were neither responsible to the voters nor even to the political parties.

Jayewardene saw, more importantly, fault with the cabinet system of government that Sri Lanka has been used to since 1947 and even before in a prototype.[49] "Our Cabinet, the executive government, is chosen from the Legislature and throughout its life is dependent on it maintaining a majority therein," he said. Then he contrasted that with the systems in the USA and France. He concluded the following which became the philosophy and the blueprint of the 1978 Constitution.[50]

Such an executive is a strong executive seated in power for a fixed number of years, not subject to the <u>whims and fancies of an elected legislature</u>; not afraid to take correct but unpopular decisions because of <u>censure from its parliamentary party</u>. This seems to me a very necessary requirement in a developing country faced with grave problems such as we are faced with today. (My emphasis).

Jayewardene was not only talking about 'whims and fancies of an elected legislature' but also the undesirable 'censure from its parliamentary party.'

Fundamental Rights

The 1978 Constitution attempted to assure what Jayewardene considered as 'basic freedoms of democracy' in a fundamental rights chapter (Chapter III). From a legal or a constitutional point of view, the rights enshrined in the chapter appeared quite impressive primarily in the sphere of civil rights except in certain areas.[51] For example, the most fundamental of all rights, the right to life was not covered in this chapter. One may argue that it is obvious or implicit in the recognition of other rights. But a clear recognition as an individual as well as a 'collective right' could have delivered a potent message in a country where the right to life became so easily extinguished in hordes even menial to the rights of animals.[52]

---

[49] In 1931, a Committee System was introduced primarily for internal self-government. The Chairmen of these Committees, seven in number, were Ministers and the Council of Ministers evolved quite akin to a modern Cabinet system after 1936. See I. D. S. Weerawardena (1951), *The Government and Politics in Ceylon, 1931-1946* (Colombo: Economic Research Association).

[50] During an interview with President Jayewardene by the present author in April 1993, he pointed out that the idea of having a strong rule, or 'Gaullist System' as he said, first became prominent during the race riots in 1958. This is confirmed by Tarzie Vittachi (1958), *Emergency '58: The Story of the Ceylon Race Riots,* London: Andre Deutsch). 'Do a de Gaulle, do a de Gaulle' was the outcry for Bandaranaike while Oliver Goonetilleke, the Governor-General, in fact acting like an executive president or a 'de Gaulle' during the riots .

[51] Even the formulations could be considered quite advanced or refined compared to for example the fundamental rights chapter in India.

[52] An individual killing of a person is well covered in law, but 'collective killings'

In addition to the fundamental rights chapter, there was a chapter on language (Chapter IV) purported to cover 'language rights' but not so much of other cultural rights. It was assumed that the political rights would be covered in the chapter on 'the people, the state and sovereignty' (Chapter 1) in addition to the chapter on franchise and elections (Chapter XIV). There was no explicit attempt to cover economic, social or even cultural rights as fundamental rights in the 1978 Constitution, except the 'free choice for an occupation' in Article 14 (1) (g). Nevertheless, some general formulations in this respect appear under the 'directive principles of state policy' along with 'fundamental duties' in Chapter VI.

There cannot be much doubt that incorporation of human rights as fundamental rights in a national constitution emerges primarily from international obligations of countries today as members of the United Nations although in the initial stages of human rights development in the world, for example in France (1789) or the United States (1791), they were national developments.[53] The incorporation of fundamental rights under international influence, however, cannot succeed unless there are commensurate national processes.[54] What could be seen by the time of the 1978 Constitution is an immense contradiction between these two processes, the international influence and the national commitment or processes. It has also to be noted that although the two international covenants on 'civil and political rights'(ICCPR) and 'economic, social and cultural rights' (ICESCR) were adopted by the United Nations in 1966, they became enforceable only in 1976 and Sri Lanka acceded to them only in January 1980. The two covenants also prescribed the state obligations to human rights differently and therefore the leaving of economic and social rights to a chapter on directive principles was understandable particularly in 1978 although this is no longer the case currently. The traditional view that economic and social rights are not justiciable is not held by many experts today.[55] Leaving that argument aside, there was no justification at all not to address the issues of 'cultural rights' or the rights of communities or

---

of people are almost unnoticed without remedy. In 1971, the killings were in thousands, in 1983 or 1987/89 in ten thousands, and thereafter, the cumulative killings in the war well exceeded hundred thousand on the part of both parties to the ethnic conflict, the armed forces and the LTTE.

[53] Sigrun I. Skogly (2006), *Beyond National Borders: State's Human Rights Obligations in International Cooperation*, (Oxford: Intersentia).

[54] Laksiri Fernando (2002), *Human Rights, Politics and States: Burma, Cambodia and Sri Lanka*, (Colombo: SSA).

[55] See Yash Ghai and Jill Cottrell, ed. (2004), *Economic, Social and Cultural Rights in Practice* (London: Interights). This study particularly focuses on South Africa.

minorities in a more positive fashion in the constitution unless there were particular reasons to neglect them or simply apply different standards to different communities and religions.

The fundamental rights chapter with Article 10 began saying "Every person is entitled to freedom of thought, conscience and religion, including the freedom to have or to adopt a religion or belief of his choice." There is no question that as passive individuals, every citizen was guaranteed freedom of religion, including adopting a religion of his or her choice. However, the said article or the article on the 'right to equality' (Article 12) failed to guarantee the much controversial equality between religions as communities or freedom therein. The latter article said "All persons are equal before the law and are entitled to the equal protection of the law" and "No citizen shall be discriminated against on the grounds of race, religion, language, caste, sex, political opinion, place of birth or any such grounds." Even here the 'equality before and protection of the law' was guaranteed to the individual but not to the religious community. The only feeble guarantee was in the article on 'freedom of speech, assembly and association' (Article 14) where it stated that "Every citizen is entitled to the freedom, either by himself or in association with others, and either in public or in private, to manifest his religion or belief in worship, observance, practice or teaching."

Like in many other countries, there had been a close connection between the State and religion in traditional Sri Lankan society. Buddhism as the predominant religion in society was often accorded the foremost place by the State or the King. It was almost the state religion. What could be seen in the 1978 Constitution, in fact beginning with the 1972 Constitution, was a resurrection of this tradition. The Constitution has a single article chapter on Buddhism (Chapter III) which very clearly sates "The Republic of Sri Lanka shall give to Buddhism the foremost place and accordingly it shall be the duty of the State to protect and foster the Buddha Sasana" adding at the end "while assuring to all religions the rights granted by Articles 10 and 14(1) (e)." As we have seen before, Article 10 or Article 14 (1) (e) intends to protect an individual's right to practice religion and not so much of protecting the religious freedom on an equal basis. This cannot be the case while granting the 'foremost place' to one religion.[56]

It is a controversial matter whether Buddhism is strictly a state religion or

---

[56] For a critical study of state religion relationship in contemporary societies from a human rights point of view see Jeroen Temperman (2010), *State-Religion Relationships and Human Rights Law* (Leiden: Martinus Nijhoff). This study raises the question of a 'right to religiously neutral governance.'

not in Sri Lanka. It is usually classified as an ambiguous state on the issue of state religion. The formulation is more subtle than in countries where there is an explicit state religion but the state's religious affiliation is undeniable. The thinking behind the foremost place for Buddhism appears to be that this special position derives from 'history' and Buddhism being the 'religion of the majority.' Both notions however are irreconcilable with 'universality' and 'equality' of modern human rights.

The controversy regarding individual rights and group rights have many dimensions. When human rights became a major challenge for many developing countries which were still largely traditional, human rights were rejected or questioned as promoting individualism.[57] In Asia, including Sri Lanka, it was argued that the Asian values were different based on communitarian concerns. Therefore, group rights were emphasized instead of individual rights. In Sri Lanka, there is an extremely peculiar ideology that governs the human rights landscape which enthrones the group rights of the majority while relegating only individual rights to the minorities. In some growing opinion, even individual rights are not fully accorded to the minorities except that they could live rather submissively. A recent most statement in this respect has come from Ven. Kirama Wimalajothi Thera, Head of the Bodu Bala Sena (BBS) expressing their opposition to the provincial council system, saying "This is a Sinhala Buddhist country and others can also live here."

The provincial council system was forced upon us. Now certain foreign groups and NGOs have started to pry on us and introduce the system to the North where there are Tamil and Muslim nationals. If this power is given to these people it will be very dangerous. Even your children and the next generation will be affected badly by this. So we are telling the President, ministers and foreign forces that we are against the 13th Amendment. This is a Sinhala Buddhist country and others can also live here. If in case they go ahead with it then they will have to introduce these powers to these areas over our dead bodies.[58] (My emphasis).

In the first Independent Constitution of 1947, there was recognition of 'religions' and 'communities' as relevant rights holders within the

---

[57] For a general penetrating discussion see Filip Spagnoli (2003), *Homo Democraticus: On the Universal Desirability and the Not So Universal Possibility of Democracy and Human Rights* (Buckinghamshire: Cambridge Scholars Press). For the particular issue see p. 230.

[58] *The Sunday Times*, Political Editor, 7 July 2013. http://www.sundaytimes.lk/130707/columns/rajapaksa-regime-bows-to-india-and-world-community-51931.html

democratic polity, although not in an elaborated fashion. This is clear from Article 29 (2). However, in that constitution which in fact was drafted even before the Universal Declaration of Human Rights (1948), there was no fundamental rights chapter. There is no doubt that even that constitution or the said Article 29 failed in defending the rights of the minorities in respect of the disenfranchisement of the Tamil plantation workers (1949) or the Sinhala Only Act (1956) due to the weaknesses of the judiciary. However, if we take the principles of Article 29 (2) seriously, it is very clear that both the chapter on Buddhism and the chapter on language are contrary to those principles. While Article 29 (1) saying "Parliament shall have power to make laws for the peace, order and good government of the Island" it also prescribed the following.

No such law shall - (a) prohibit or restrict the free exercise of any religion; or (b) make persons of any community or religion liable to disabilities or restrictions to which persons of other communities or religions are not made liable; or (c) confer on persons of any community or religion any privilege or advantage which is not conferred on persons of other communities or religions.

The original 1978 Constitution, exactly like the 1972 Constitution, conferred that "The Official Language of Sri Lanka shall be Sinhala" in Article 18. Only difference from the previous constitution was that it conferred a national language status to the Tamil language saying "The National Languages of Sri Lanka shall be Sinhala and Tamil" in Article 19. However it was not clear that what would constitute a 'national language.' It was initially confined mainly to the use of either Sinhalese or Tamil in parliamentary proceedings and the administrative use of both languages. It was the 16th Amendment to the Constitution that clarified the matter to a great extent. The rights related to language however is an area where a considerable progress could be seen under the 1978 Constitution. There were 14 insertions and substitutions to the chapter on language. In contrast, there had been no amendments at all to the chapter on fundamental rights. However, some of the insertions were not only ambiguous but also demeaning. For example, the initial constitution said "The official language of Sri Lanka shall be Sinhala" and then the 13th Amendment added that "Tamil shall also be an official language."[59]

Practice of Fundamental Rights

---

[59] It was like saying, 'this is my wife' and saying with a chuckle 'this is also my wife.' There was still a hierarchical order between the languages of Sinhala and Tamil.

There is no dispute that there were good things in the fundamental rights chapter and for example, "No person shall be subjected to torture or to cruel, inhuman or degrading treatment or punishment." However, torture is the most prevalent day to day human rights violation in Sri Lanka according to a number of human rights reports and irrespective of the fact that there is other legislation prohibiting the same, not to speak of 'cruel, inhuman or degrading treatment.'[60] The main perpetrator identified is obviously the police. In the implementation of the right to freedom from torture what could be mostly seen is the lack of political commitment on the part of political authorities in charge of the police and the armed forces. The efforts of the judiciary in this respect are largely hampered or circumscribed because of the negative interference and the defense of the perpetrators by the Attorney General's Department. This is irrespective Sri Lanka being party to the Convention Against Torture (CAT) since 1994 and has its own Convention Against Torture Act (1994).

The same goes for the "freedom from arbitrary arrest, detention and punishment." The article on the subject (Article 13), to appear in any constitution, is most comprehensive with seven sections. The principles enunciated are very close to what appears in the ICCPR or other international instruments. However, arbitrary arrest and detention are other two prevalent human rights violations in Sri Lanka apart from and leading to torture even after the end of the war in 2009. During the period of war between 1983 and 2009, there were legally sanctioned possibilities under the emergency laws and the much controversial Prevention of Terrorism Act (PTA) that made the provisions in the constitution only theoretical and abundantly redundant. The same Article 13 also prohibited 'retroactive penal legislation' which by and large Sri Lanka has complied with. However, on the other hand Article 16 validated the operation of "all existing written law and unwritten law...notwithstanding any inconsistency with the preceding provisions of this Chapter" to mean the fundamental rights chapter. Most of the legal ambiguities regarding the cases of torture or arbitrary arrest/detention came about because of the above 'indemnity.' The existing Police Ordinance for example allowed many arbitrary actions including coerced treatment in the process of law enforcement.[61]

---

[60] Asian Human Rights Commission (AHRC) compiled a report of 1,500 cases of torture between 1998 and 2011, "A Review of Sri Lanka's Compliance with the Obligations under CAT," 8 July 2011. See other publications of AHRC including *Torture* magazine.

[61] Laksiri Fernando (2005), *Police-Civil Relations for Good Governance* (Colombo: SSA).

Article 14 of the fundamental rights chapter was quite wide ranging to include not only the 'freedom of speech, assembly and association' but also as it declared the "the freedom to engage by himself or in association with others in any lawful occupation, profession, trade, business or enterprise," which in fact touched on economic rights. However, as it was couched within the other civil rights associated with the freedom of expression or association, its importance or relevance escaped the attention of even the judicious commentators. The article most importantly recognized (a) the freedom of speech and expression including publication; (b) the freedom of peaceful assembly; (c) the freedom of association; and (d) the freedom to form and join a trade union.

In all these areas, Sri Lanka had a strong tradition and even practice until these rights became increasingly impinged due to political circumstances or expediency in fact associated with the introduction of the presidential system. Otherwise Sri Lanka was one of the best countries that respected and allowed the entertainment of these rights unimpaired. The lives of governments previously largely depended on the acceptance of these rights. Two examples could be given conveniently. In 1953, a Prime Minister opted to resign consequence of 13 lives lost during trade union protest and civil disobedience. In 1964, a government was defeated in a parliament when it attempted to nationalize a major newspaper establishment, the Lake House.[62] On the other hand, these are the kinds of predicaments that J. R. Jayewardene wanted to terminate by introducing a presidential system in the country.

The major merit of the fundamental rights chapter of the 1978 Constitution was its justiciability compared to the 1972 Constitution, and according to which "every person shall be entitled to apply to the Supreme Court, as provided by Article 126, in respect of the infringement or imminent infringement, by executive or administrative action." Article 126 in addition allowed the same procedure for the language rights recognized in Chapter III although this procedure has not been very much used.[63] The fundamental rights implementation procedure was obviously limited to the 'executive or administrative action' in the public sector (private sector excluded) although extended to the 'infringement or imminent infringement.' While there was no redress given if any fundamental or

---

[62] For the general character of democracy during the period see James Jupp (1978), *Sri Lanka: Third World Democracy* (London: Frank Cass).

[63] See Theva Rajan (1995), *Tamil as Official Language: Retrospect and Prospect* (Colombo: ICES).

language right was infringed by the judiciary, the collective human rights violations related to events or incidents (i.e. burning of the Jaffna Library, July 1983 riots, Anuradhapura massacre by the LTTE or election violence) were completely beyond the purview of judicial investigation and determination.[64] In initial judgements it was also determined that only persons and not entities such as media institutions, companies or trade unions that could apply for redress. This was made flexible later.

Under the prevailing provisions, the most operational fundamental rights jurisdiction was related to the 'right to equality' under Article 12. Petitioners applied to the Supreme Court when their rights became infringed due to punishments, transfers, denial of promotion or other discriminatory action in the public sector including the police service, which could easily be handled by an Equal Opportunity Commission or even the current National Human Rights Commission, if it is constituted impartially and professionally.[65] Discrimination or denial of opportunity in education also became a prominent form of fundamental rights cases before the Supreme Court in recent times. The major fall out as a result was the escape of most important human rights violations from the judicial scrutiny. Media Reform Lanka linked to the Institute of Commonwealth Studies, University of London, however recorded selected 26 cases related to the freedom of speech and expression from 1983 to 2003.[66]

The fundamental rights issues and cases have undoubtedly been a learning process for the country and the judiciary alike. Initially, there was a failure to grasp the fundamental rights within the broader framework of international human rights, or the organized entities as relevant rights holders. However, this position substantially became altered later. The Saturday Review was disadvantaged in 1984 on the basis that only individuals and not entities who could apply when it filed two petitions against the sealing of the press. But The Sunday Leader benefitted when the prohibition of publication by the Competent Authority was challenged in 2000. As our list shows, the first decade (1980s) shows a dismal prospect for fundamental rights cases perhaps due to the political climate as well judges being quite conservative or not so knowledgeable about human

---

[64] This author believes that constitutional provisions could be formulated to initiate compulsory judicial investigations into collective or mass killings or similar human rights violations.

[65] Although the appointments to the Human Rights Commission were done on an impartial basis prior to around 2005, in recent times partisan affiliations have become the main criteria of appointment.

[66] "Excerpts from Relevant Sri Lankan Case Law on Freedom of Expression and freedom of the Media," http://mediareformlanka.com/Cases.pdf

rights issues. Even their determinations were quite scanty and contradictory if you go through the determinations.

The situation however improved in the second decade (1990s). Although the involvement of the highest executive authorities in the infringements were continued to be the case, it did appear that the judiciary was quite confident in delivering their determinations independently. Some of the politically prominent cases of Jana Gosha, Ratawesi Peramuna, Yukthiya or the UNP May Day were determined in favor of the petitioners. Another positive development was to interpret the freedom of speech and expression as broadly as possible even to include the right to vote within its purview. The determinations of the judges also were quite extensive, yet these cases were an extremely small fraction of the incidents of systemic human rights violations going on in the country during the period.

Moreover they confined mainly to the rights of certain sections or individuals in the South as if the Northern parts of the country were completely debarred from the fundamental rights process. For some reason, not a single known case was filed under the language rights. As a whole, it appeared that the fundamental rights procedure was like trying to fish (or not to fish) big sharks with a small net. The major incidents of rights violations in July 1980, July 1983, 1987-89 or during the four Eelam wars including the last stages in 2009 have completely escaped any judicial scrutiny inside the country. No other mechanisms or devices were installed, except for few efforts such as the Commissions on Disappearances in 1995, as a way of ameliorating the ongoing saga. None of the cases listed or others, as they were part of systemic and endemic nature, could be considered 'pilot cases' where the causes of violations were identified and instructed the state authorities to prevent those in the future suggesting necessary measures.[67] The reason for this situation was largely determined by the connection between the system of government and the human rights violations. No need to repeat that the Presidential System was by and large responsible.

Failure of a System

---

[67] Since 2004 the European Court adopted a procedure to take up only 'pilot cases' or deliver 'pilot judgements' focusing on causes as well as recommendations to curtail systemic violations. See Philip Leach et al (2010), *Responding to Systemic Human Rights Violations* (New York: Angus and Robertson). A similar procedure could have been or could be adopted by the Supreme Court in Sri Lanka leaving other cases for example to the Human Rights Commission or any other court.

There was some flexibility in the state system before the 1978 Constitution or more precisely before the 1972 Constitution in dealing with the ethnic question or any other human rights issue. Moreover, the major violations during the period were few and far between.[68] But the state now became restrictively defined as a 'unitary state,' to mean centralized, vertical and even authoritarian.[69] The 'unitary state' has also become a frenzied slogan on the part of the extreme Sinhala nationalists. What became precluded were the development of horizontal democratic institutions and processes and even the implementation of devolution under the 13th Amendment becoming subjected to continuous upheavals as a result.

On 'the people, the state and sovereignty,' (Chapter I) first the state was defined as 'free, sovereign and independent.' This may be necessary, though obvious, as freedom could exist only in a free state as Rousseau argued. Sri Lanka as a former colony, this was also necessary to assert its sovereignty and independence from the former colonial master or any other similar source. But the definition of the state as 'unitary' placed an untold internal restrictions from which it would be extremely difficult to extricate itself. The 1978 Constitution also added that Sri Lanka is a 'democratic socialist republic' whatever it meant. Even the 1972 Constitution did not have this characterization although drafted by a group of socialists. The economic path that was taken in 1977 with the inauguration of an 'open economic policy' was hardly akin to any type of socialism. Only reason that can be adduced to this characterization was that perhaps the founder of the constitution wanted to pass the message that democracy under the 1978 Constitution was only a qualified one. It was a known fact that the 'democratic socialist' countries in Eastern Europe were prominently authoritarian not to speak of the East Asian socialist countries.

One of the advantages for any human rights movement in the country, however, was the broad and popular definition given to the notion of sovereignty. In the 1972 Constitution it said "In the Republic of Sri Lanka sovereignty is in the people and is inalienable" and then the 1978 Constitution added that "Sovereignty includes the powers of government, fundamental rights and the franchise." The new inclusion of 'fundamental

---

[68] If the number of killings, unfortunately, were an indication of major human rights violations, then until 1971 it was relatively a period of calm. At a general strike in 1947, one was killed and 18 injured. In a Hartal in 1953, 13 were killed and over 200 were injured. During two racial riots in 1956 and 1958, 158 and over 500 were reported to be killed respectively. But in contrast, 1971 saw over 5,000 killed and 12,000 arrested. It was a story of escalation.

[69] For a discussion on the unitary state and for its evolution see A. J. Wilson (1988), *The Break-Up of Sri Lanka: The Sinhalese-Tamil Conflict* (London: C. Hurst).

rights and the franchise' within the purview of sovereignty perhaps indicated that the drafters of the constitution, including President Jayewardene, didn't consciously anticipate that the system of government that they were installing might go against the fundamental rights in the constitution. In addition to the inclusion of fundamental rights in the people's sovereignty it further said "the fundamental rights which are by the Constitution declared and recognized shall be respected, secured and advanced by all the organs of government, and shall not be abridged, restricted or denied, save in the manner and to the extent hereinafter provided."

In view of the strong recognition of fundamental rights in the constitution it is puzzling to see how did the executive branch of the government (i.e. the police, the armed forces, the bureaucracy, competent authorities, attorney general's department etc.) could trample on human rights of the people or why did the other branches of the government (primarily the legislative and the judicial) or even the people allowed major violations to take place committed by both the state and non-state actors.[70] The answer to this question may need to take into consideration a host of factors and primarily, political, constitutional and social. That kind of a broader analysis also requires different approaches encompassing ideological and even psychological. Then the question remains as to the failure of the international institutions and primarily the UN in protecting the rights of the people in Sri Lanka when the gross human rights violations took place.

To highlight one facet in respect of the social, it appears that major violations continued unopposed by the people depending on the ethnic, political, religious, class and even caste affiliations or biases. The passivity of the people in the midst of gross violations cannot be explained merely by the repressive nature of the government or the armed forces. While some of these biases encompassed the ideological sphere, some others were psychological. For example, when violations took place in the North, the people in the South were indifferent or rejoiced and vice versa. The same partialities or silence occurred on religious, political or other distinctions.[71]

---

[70] Some of the initial studies were: Nihal Jayawickrema (1976), *Human Rights in Sri Lanka* (Berkeley: University of California); Patricia Hyndman (1992), *Human Rights Accountability in Sri Lanka* (New York: Human Rights Watch). For a Bibliography for the initial period, see Kumar Rupesinghe and Berth Verstappen (1989), *Ethnic Conflict and Human Rights in Sri Lanka: An Annotated Bibliography* (Oslo: Hans Zell). There are extensive reports available from UTHR (J), CRM, INFORM, Amnesty International, Human Rights Watch, ICJ, Minority Rights Group, Article 19 etc.

[71] It is possible to speculate that many of the partialities and discrimination

The same partialities or biases remained within the governing institutions and among the personnel who were manning those institutions. However, our effort in this chapter has been limited and primarily to identify the discernible constitutional factors in relation to the major violations of human rights during the period. All these factors together constitute a systemic failure in its broadest sense of the term.

There was a major dislocation in the representative democracy in Sri Lanka when the executive was separated and elevated from the Parliament with considerable implications on human rights. A widely elected parliament on the basis of universal franchise should not only be the legislative branch but also the base and 'mother' of the executive. The executive should sit in parliament and should answer, responsible and be accountable. Separation and full independence are necessary only for the judiciary to safeguard the constitutional rights of the people and administer justice. It may be argued that Baron Montesquieu got the priorities mixed up when he proposed a strict system of separation of powers in the mid-18th century. His reading of the English constitutional system was erroneous for the evolving reality than for the archaic past.[72] When the United States applied the separation of powers in its constitution, the purpose was not to create a strong executive or president but to institute separation between the three branches and also to create checks and balances. The initial Presidents of America were liberal leaders and a strong presidential system evolved much later.[73] However, this was not the case when France devised its own presidential system in 1958 under General Charles de Gaulle. The purpose was to install an authoritarian rule like the 'future Sri Lanka' and in fact J. R. Jayewardene took inspiration from the Gaullist system.[74] Another trace of the 1978 Constitution was the ancient monarchical system as Mervyn de Silva argued and this trait of monarchical thinking still prevails in the country.

Its main feature was an unparalleled concentration of power in the presidency. While foreign scholars termed the new system 'Bonapartist-Gaullist' or a 'benevolent authoritarianism,' its architect rejoiced, saying that

---

based on hierarchical thinking is a reincarnation of archaic caste system in the Sri Lankan society and tradition.

[72] Chapter 6 of Book XI of *The Spirit of the Laws*.

[73] Woodrow Wilson was a major critic of separation of powers and the presidential system. Both his amateur work *Congressional Government* and the mature *Constitutional Government* develops the same line of thinking in appreciation of parliamentary system.

[74] A. J. Wilson (1980), *The Gaullist System in Asia: The Constitution of Sri Lanka 1978*, (London: Palgrave Macmillan).

he was 'more powerful than King Parakramabahu the Great.[75]

The sovereignty of the people however was the catch word to install the authoritarian system and Article 4 was the basic framework for its architecture. First it said "the legislative power of the People shall be exercised by Parliament, consisting of elected representatives of the People and by the People at a Referendum." It should be noted, however, that although 'referendum' was named as a devise of exercising 'legislative power' of the people, there had been only one referendum so far in December 1982 which was alleged to be fraudulent and ironically that was to extend the term of the incumbent parliament for another six years without holding the due parliamentary election in 1983.[76] The Parliament also was unicameral without any possibility of allowing the electorally unrepresented and deserving people to serve the country in legislative matters in a second chamber. For democracy to operate properly, it is always better to balance the functions of a house of representatives with a second chamber. Under the devolution of power to the provinces in 1987, a second chamber could have served as a conduit for power sharing at the center. The Senate that operated under the first independent constitution until it was abolished in 1971 was a center where public issues were debated beyond partisan politics and almost served as an informal human rights council.[77]

The following was what the Constitution said about the executive branch of government in the framework section (Chapter I).

"The executive power of the People including the defense of Sri Lanka, shall be exercised by the President of the Republic elected by the People."

Here there was no mentioning of a Cabinet or a Prime Minister and those provisions came in Chapter VIII clearly implying they were subordinate to the President. The purpose of the Cabinet of Ministers was to serve the President not as an independent body but as a subordinate entity. It further explained that the President "is the Head of the State, the Head of the Executive and of the Government, and the Commander-in-Chief of the Armed Forces." There is no dispute that the 1978 Constitution retained

---

[75] "Repression in the Guise of Stability," *International Herald Tribune*, 23 April1986.

[76] While no election was held for the Parliament between 1977 and 1988, the local government system also was frozen during the same period with major consequences for the representative democracy.

[77] I. D. S. Weerawardena (1955), *The Senate of Ceylon at Work* (Peradeniya: University of Ceylon).

certain aspects of a parliamentary system not as a mixture like in France but side by side. This is clear from the provisions in Chapter VIII. This has been more beneficial for the preservation of some semblance of parliamentary democracy than a mixed system like in France. During December 2001 and April 2004, when the Parliament was elected from a different political party to that of the President, the country could revert back to almost a cabinet system of government. This could happen as the incumbent President, opted not to use her immense executive powers until the last moment. This was also the period of the peace process and the Ceasefire Agreement (CFA) when gross human rights violations became reduced although one could argue that the uncertainty and conflict between the President and the Prime Minister contributed to the failure of the peace process in addition to the LTTE abusing the peace process for their military objectives. This supports our main argument, however, that a cabinet system of government is more conducive to human rights and peace, if unhampered by any semblance of a presidential system.

The presidential system in Sri Lanka has been more authoritarian internally than most the other presidential systems in the world, particularly the US or France, and given the long tenure of office it could easily be abused. The term of office is six years and initially the terms were limited to two, until the 18th Amendment in September 2010. Compared to the four year term in the US, this meant that a President in Sri Lanka could serve (if elected of course) for a period similar to three terms in the US. Now the term limit is lifted and in theory one could become a lifetime president. In France, the period was seven years earlier but now limited to five and also prohibiting anyone serving more than two consecutive terms. In the US, although there was no two term limit until the 22nd Amendment in 1947, only four Presidents attempted to contest for more than two terms and only Franklin D. Roosevelt succeeded under the special circumstances of the war. Although in Russia the period of term is six years like in Sri Lanka, the office is limited to two consecutive terms. Moreover, the Russian President is not the head of the executive branch. In almost all countries, while the trend has been to limit the terms and even powers of the President, Sri Lanka is a country which has moved in the opposite direction. The 3rd Amendment to the Constitution made the matters much worse by allowing the President to seek a new mandate after the expiration of four years, nevertheless continuing the previous term for the full period and then commencing the current after that if elected. This virtually meant that eight year period could be mandated by one election.

The Presidents also have acquired glory and power through convention and ideology.[78] In a country where the traditional kingship was suppressed by colonialism and many people still yearn for that traditional glory and myth, the position of the President was the only institution that it could be invoked. The first President J. R. Jayewardene fully benefitted from this aura whether he truly believed it or not. He claimed to be more powerful than some of the most powerful kings of the past and said he could do anything other than 'making a man a woman or woman a man.' The same invincibility is resurrected under the current President as well. This is partly because of the almost complete immunity given by the Constitution itself in Article 35 (1) which says, "While any person holds office as President, no proceedings shall he instituted or continued against him in any court or tribunal in respect of anything done or omitted to be done by him either in his official or private capacity." Although constitutional analysts opined that this could not mean any immunity at least to breach the Constitution, in a situation of subdued judiciary it had extremely been difficult to challenge any of the actions of the Presidents in a court of law.[79] The President also cannot be removed during his/her tenure other than by an extremely difficult procedure of impeachment.

The main casualty under the presidential system was the independence of the judiciary with considerable human rights implications. The downturn started with the 1972 Constitution on a different trajectory. On the assumption of the supremacy of Parliament, the judiciary was made subordinate and even it retained some judicial power of its own. The retention continued under the 1978 Constitution although the Parliament was no longer supreme. The encroachment on the judiciary came in a different manner. In spite of the nominal Head of State, of course on the advice of the Prime Minister, appointing the judges of the superior courts, under the 1978 Constitution, the appointments of the Supreme Court and the Court of Appeal came under the direct discretion of the Executive President. Article 107 (1) said "The Chief Justice, the President of the Court of Appeal and every other Judge, of the Supreme Court and Court of Appeal shall be appointed by the President of the Republic by warrant under his hand." It was under this article that the all sitting judges of the superior courts had to resign and reappointed with a significant reshuffle. It was barely three years before in August 1985 that the UN enunciated the

---

[78] The situation is quite akin to Oriental Despotism that Wittfogel depicted. Karl Wittfogel (1967), *Oriental Despotism: A Comparative Study of Total Power* (London: Yale University Press). See also Laksiri Fernando, "Karl Marx, Asiatic Despotism and Sri Lanka," *Colombo Telegraph*, 13 March 2013.

[79] See Basil Fernando, "Sri Lanka: The Need to Re-interpret the Executive President's Impunity under Article 35 (1)," Asian Human Rights Commission, 14 November 2012.

"Basic Principles on the Independence of the Judiciary" where the independence of the judiciary was emphasized in terms of rule of law and human rights in the Preamble as well as in the substantive articles. The most important principles were the following.

"The independence of the judiciary shall be guaranteed by the State and enshrined in the Constitution or the law of the country. It is the duty of all governmental and other institutions to respect and observe the independence of the judiciary. The judiciary shall decide matters before them impartially, on the basis of facts and in accordance with the law, without any restrictions, improper influences, inducements, pressures, threats or interferences, direct or indirect, from any quarter or for any reason."[80]

Within months of the promulgation of the 1978 Constitution, the Special Presidential Commission Law no 7 of 1978 was enacted with the purpose depriving the former Prime Minister, Sirimavo Bandaranaike, of her civic rights. When the Court of Appeal declared, on an application, that the retrospective application of the law was null and void, the President decided to change the Constitution and make the purview of the Commission applicable retrospectively and also pruning the powers of the Court of Appeal. The deprivation of civic rights of Mrs Bandaranaike was the first major human rights issue under the 1978 Constitution. It is reported that President Jayewardene had said "the judiciary would pose difficulties for the executive if they are wholly outside anyone's control."[81]

There had been a trail of events since 1978 that accompanied the suppression of democracy, violation of human rights and silencing of the judiciary which went hand in hand. The attempt here is not to give a full record but highlight some initial key events. First it was the deprivation of civic rights of the foremost potential challenger to the presidential position in 1978 itself. Handpicked three judges were conveniently used in the exercise. In 1981, the Jaffna District Council election was blatantly manipulated with violence and that was a part and parcel of coercing the emerging minority opposition in the North.[82] Orders had been already given to General Tissa Weeratunga to 'eliminate terrorism completely from the Northern soil' with additional powers given under the draconian Prevention of Terrorism Act (1979). The confrontations continued with the full explosion of July 1983 violence against the ethnic Tamils with colossal damage to property, life and ethnic relations in the country. Nearly a million

---

[80] U.N. Doc. A/CONF. 121/22Rev. 1 at 59 (1985).

[81] Ambika Satkunanathan, "Working of Democracy in Sri Lanka," [Monograph, LST]. http://www.democracy-asia.org/qa/srilanka/Ambika

[82] See Nancy Murray, "The State against Tamils," *Race & Class*, XXVI, 1 (1984).

of Tamils were driven out of the country.[83] That was the beginning of the Eelam War I which lasted until 1985. The connection between the suppression of democracy, the violation of human rights and the silencing of the judiciary has continued until this day, the latest most example for the latter being the impeachment of the Chief Justice Dr Shirani Bandaranayake in 2012.

Conclusion

This chapter did not make any substantive effort to record the events and incidents of human rights violations during the period since the 1978 Constitution and these are available in a multitude of sources, national and international, as referred to before. Instead, the effort was to isolate the key constitutional factors that were primarily responsible, in author's opinion, for the protection and promotion of human rights violations within a context of increasing conflicts of ethnic and/or political nature.

If this chapter started with the hypothesis that parliamentary democracies in contrast to the presidential systems are more conducive to human rights protection based on the views of Karel Vasak, this hypothesis became substantially substantiated by the end of the chapter both on empirical and constitutional premises. The fundamental rights chapter in the 1978 Constitution could not hold water. On the empirical side of the equation, it is abundantly clear that major violations started to escalate under the Presidential rule, individual presidents making matters worse both by commission and omission although this second aspect was not pursued very much in this chapter given the space constraints. The Parliamentary period of the constitutional history of the country (1948-1978) in contrast was in fact was a 'golden age' except certain aberrations under the 1972 Constitution. This hypothesis again became confirmed by the fact that the period between 2001 and 2004 was largely favorable to human rights and peace when the system temporarily reverted back to the old system of Cabinet government as we have shown. This was also the period when the Independent Commissions existed under the 17th Amendment.

Human rights violations primarily emerge in any country from the state apparatuses (or from movements driving towards creating such apparatuses i.e. the LTTE in Sri Lanka) if those apparatuses are not governed by democratic rule of law. Violators are not usually the civil society actors. As Karl Marx maintained:

---

[83] A Jeyaratnam Wilson gave some direct evidence for the government involvement in the 1983 riots. *The Break-up of Sri Lanka,* 1988, p. 173.

"Freedom consists in the conversion of the State from an organ superimposed on society into one completely subordinated to it, and today too, the forms of the State are more free or less free to the extent that they restrict the 'freedom' of the State."[84]

The state apparatuses encompass the armed forces, the police, the prisons and the bureaucracy in various forms and shapes. The handling of this 'monster' is primarily a task of the executive branch of the modern government and the best handling of this task conducive to human rights would be if the executive branch is directly and intimately responsible and accountable to an elected Parliament of the people and this means primarily a parliamentary system of government. While this is a necessary condition for the protection and promotion of human rights it is also not a sufficient condition. There are other socio-political, cultural, ideological and institutional conditions necessary although this study did not go into details of them.

As we could observe from our analysis and descriptions, when the executive branch of the government in the form of executive presidency became divorced from the legislator and in fact dominates both the legislator and the judiciary through various means that was not conducive to human rights. Much worse was the situation when the President received a separate mandate overriding the mandate of the Parliament and believed in authoritarian government for the sake ostensibly for developing the country economically in a situation where the understanding or resolve to defend human rights was not so high even within the civil society. This might not totally be the case if the presidential system was accompanied by extensive checks and balances and if the society or the economy is developed. But in a developing or a transitional country like in Sri Lanka, the presidential system did spell disaster for human rights and civil liberties as we could observe from the past experience. The main motivation to undertake this study was our observation of an evolving debate in Sri Lanka at present on the subject of whether the presidential or parliamentary democracy is the better system for human rights and democracy. However, as Matthew S. Shugart and John M. Carey said, "Most of the scholarly literature on the subject comes out quite squarely behind parliamentarism as the preferred alternative. However, among practicing politicians, the message is getting through slowly, if at all."[85]

---

[84] Quoted by Perry Anderson (1974), *Lineages of the Absolutist State* (London: Verso), p. 11.

[85] Matthew S. Shugart and John M. Carey, op. cit. p. 2.

3
Why Do We Need a New Constitution?

"The dead should not rule the living." - Thomas Jefferson

Constitution making in a polarized society is not an easy task. I prefer to use the term 'polarized' than a 'divided or a deeply divided society,' with a cautiously optimistic note. Sri Lanka unfortunately is still polarized not only in ethnic but also in political terms, like many other countries in the region. However, as the two elections last year (presidential in January and parliamentary in August) and the current 'national unity' government, of course mainly the UNP and the SLFP, show there are some possible consensus on a New Constitution, yet uneasy.

Seemingly broad consensus, particularly among the people, appear to be on 'democracy' or 'furtherance of democracy,' after changing a difficultly entrenched 'authoritarian regime' in 2015. This also implied 'justice to the minority communities' and 'resolution of the ethnic conflict,' although those did not come to the forefront automatically at elections. Suspicions, old notions or determination to keep 'majority rule' are still lingering. The government has declared three major areas of reform for a New Constitution. As the Prime Minister, Ranil Wickremesinghe, has outlined at the Sujata Jayawardena Oration (11 December 2015):

The Cabinet Committee on Constitutional Reforms has already, in consultation with the Leaders of Parties in Parliament, decided to appoint a Public Representation Commission which will obtain the views of the public and forward a Report to the Constitutional Assembly by 31st March

2016. Today, the three main issues before the Constitutional Assembly are: Devolution, the electoral system and the alternative to the Executive Presidency.[86]

Devolution undoubtedly is a priority in this effort. As Hanna Lerner (*Making Constitutions in Deeply Divided Societies*, 2013) has said, "In recent years constitutions have become a leading tool for mitigating conflicts and promoting democracy in divided societies." South Africa is one good example.

Why Need a New?

If democratic change is achieved, as claimed, why do we need a new constitution? One may ask. To consolidate the achievements and move further, could be one answer. Joseph Stalin (who has never been in my good books) gave an important answer in justifying the need for a new constitution in the Soviet Union in 1936. He said that 'the necessity for a new constitution arose from changes in the country that transpired since the previous constitution of 1924.' The essence of this answer is equally valid at least partly for the need for a new constitution in Sri Lanka today. Much water and also 'dead bodies' have flowed under the bridge since 1978. The changes have been both negative and positive. Although all the reasons for the war or terrorism, including the southern ones, cannot be blamed on the 1978 constitution, the system in place (an authoritarian President at the helm) was not conducive in mitigating or seeking an early solution. The economy became largely stagnated, mostly lopsided with vast social disparities. The final outcome of the constitutional setup was the Rajapaksa family rule, emerging as an obnoxious authoritarian regime. The various promises to change the constitution and abolish the presidential system since 1994 did not materialize within the vicious cycle. Now there is a chance to break the cycle, and move beyond. The defects were/are systemic and not personal alone.

Changes in the country after 1978, and particularly recently, were not all negative, although partial. There are new generations of youth who have emerged with more liberal values, different to the values of the older generations. Even in the constitutional sphere, the 13th and the 17th Amendments were major achievements, the first creating a base for

---

[86] It should be mentioned that some of the terminology have changed. The Constitutional Assembly is now called the Constituent Assembly and the Public Representation Commission is now named the Public Representation Committee.

effective devolution, and the second establishing independent commissions to free the public services, the judiciary, the police etc. from political interferences and control. However, the 17th was reversed in 2010 and the 13th also was circumscribed under the presidential rule and due to other structural defects. Some of the fundamental flaws of the 1978 initial document became revealed by having 16 amendments within first ten years; and one even not enacted. The 16th Amendment also was a good one on language use, although not put into proper practice. There was no amendment, unfortunately, similar to the Article 29 in the 1947 constitution. It is not merely the number of amendments that showed the weaknesses of the constitutional structure, but their erratic or 'back and forth' character. There are fundamental defects, disparities, uncertainties and contradictions in the present text of the constitution that needs to be harmonized through a new constitution.

For the Future

Stalin was only partially or half correct in explaining the purpose of a constitution. He was so adamant, like many leftists, saying that 'a constitution should reflect the gains of a society and not the aims.' This is disputed by the liberal tradition of constitutional making. Aims and future objectives are important. The liberal tradition fundamentally looks for the future from the present. This however should not disregard the achievements. Only a lasting constitution can be made only by mixing the two. A constitution should be both the 'mirror and the mold of a polity, and also a society.'

The twin purposes (mirroring and molding) could be the guiding principles in formulating provisions in the three main areas that the PM has outlined: 'devolution,' 'electoral reform' and the 'executive system.' There are many other areas like 'fundamental rights,' 'principles of state policy,' 'arrangements for financial accountability,' 'check and balances for good governance' that these twin principles should equally apply. Simply saying, there should be a future vision. Temptations for immediate 'political advantage' should be eschewed with. Even in the 19th Amendment, there are some 'pragmatic' or more correctly 'opportunist' provisions. The failed 2000 constitutional draft is a good lesson not to indulge in petty-power-schemes. American constitution of 1787 in this sense was exemplary. It was futurist and was written in plain language. James Madison who is undisputed as a most important founder of the constitution often used the term 'America's destiny,' also to include its economic future. In deliberating on the tasks of constitutional drafting he said the following.

"In framing a government which is to be administered by men over men, the great difficulty lies in this: you must enable the government to control the governed; and in the next place oblige itself to control itself."

During the over 225 years in the US, there are only 27 amendments. Ten of them were within few years to incorporate a Bill of Rights but not to change the existing provisions. There were only few amendments since then. There was no attempt to overwrite the matters. The judiciary was allowed to interpret; and the institutions were allowed to evolve. This does not mean that everything went in the right direction, but stability and sustainability prevailed. In the Sri Lankan context, this may be too idealistic to expect. Therefore, there is nothing wrong in a detailed document, however, a lasting vision is important.

If a constitution is not framed for the future, it is doomed to fail. This is what happened in France, having five republican constitutions since 1789. This weakness was there in the 1972 Sri Lankan constitution although it was drafted well. The purpose of changing the 1947 constitution was different. The 1978 constitution has lasted for more years than the 1972 because of its rigidity and for other reasons. Sri Lanka is now poised to go for a third republican constitution, and if it fails in its future vision, it also would fail as a constitution. Another important element is forging consensus. Consensus does not necessarily mean all agree. It is impossible in the present Sri Lankan context, given the niggling power interests and schemes. However, the main stakeholders should be able to 'give and take' and 'compromise.' But this should be done on the basis of 'principles, justice and morals' and not on 'power interests.' In my opinion, it is wrong to consider what has to be resolved, particularly in the case of the ethnic conflict, is a 'power problem.' If the constitution is drafted on a future vision, justifiable on ethical, moral and practical grounds, it would last and it would be easily approved by *'We the people.'*

The Road Map

The PM, apparently as the primary mover of the New Constitution, has put forward a 'draft resolution' to be tabled before Parliament on 9 January. It gives a feasible road map for making a New Constitution. The opening clause says the following.

"There shall be a Committee of Parliament hereinafter referred to as the 'Constitutional Assembly' which shall consist of all Members of Parliament, for the purpose of deliberating on, and seeking the views and advice of the people, on a new constitution for Sri Lanka, and preparing a draft of a

Constitution Bill for the consideration of Parliament in the exercise of its powers under Article 75 of the Constitution."

The resolution is clearly written and contains cohesive 39 clauses. Clarity is important in constitution making. As it is clear from the above paragraph, a Committee of Parliament will sit as a 'Constitutional Assembly.' This is important. As I happened to advocate 12 years ago at an interview (Sunday Observer, 30 May 2004), "The benefits of a Constituent Assembly are many because the process is more democratic. In a Constituent Assembly there is no division between parties, no atmosphere for confrontation, parties will consider questions differently, rules of procedure will be different, seating arrangement is different and the members will participate as representatives of the people." I had called it a 'constituent assembly,' following the vocabulary of that time, but it is equally correct to call it a 'constitutional assembly' today.

The main tasks of the Constitutional Assembly (CA) would be (1) to deliberate on a New Constitution, (2) to seek views and advice of the people for the above, and (3) to prepare a draft of a Constitutional Bill for the consideration of Parliament. Then Parliament will exercise its powers under Article 75 of the Constitution in deliberating on it. Hopefully, there will be no legal hurdles in the process. The resolution also outlines the secretarial and organizational arrangements for the CA. There shall be sub-committees of the CA. There shall be a Steering Committee to steer the deliberations, to conduct necessary consultations, and then for the nitty gritty drafting. All the inputs from other sub-committees would come to that. The proceedings of the CA will be open to the public. An important link between the CA and the public will be the 'Public Representation Commission.' It shall setup and maintain a website and use other appropriate methods, towards giving due publicity to the process. Most importantly, it will also be the main conveyer belt of people's submissions to the Constitutional Assembly.

It is the Steering Committee which is tasked to submit a 'final report' and a 'resolution on a draft constitution.' However, there is no time frame given at the moment. The procedure is outlined in detail in adopting and/or amending the draft (Clause 26). For example, "If two-thirds of the Constitutional Assembly does not approve the resolution on the draft Constitution, the Constitutional Assembly and the Committees referred to in this Resolution shall stand dissolved." The legal or the constitutional procedure outlined in the draft resolution is not discussed here. On its face value, it appears feasible and constitutional. The procedure also includes the submission of the draft after it becomes a "Bill to every Provincial Council, and seek their views as required by Article 154G (2) of the Constitution." Then comes the referendum.

To Dispel Doubts

It is important to quote in full the two last clauses of the draft resolution 'to dispel any doubt' about the legality or the constitutionality of the procedure outlined.

38. For the avoidance of doubt, it is hereby declared that the adoption or rejection or adoption subject to amendment of such a draft Constitution as proposed by the Constitutional Assembly, shall be the responsibility of Parliament.

39. For the avoidance of doubt it is hereby further declared that a Constitution Bill shall only be enacted into law if it is passed in Parliament by a special majority of 2/3 of the whole number of the Members of Parliament, including those not present and subsequently approved by the people at a Referendum as required by Article 83 of the Constitution.

The effort to draft and adopt a New Constitution is consistent with the mandate of President Maithripala Sirisena, at the presidential elections on 7 January 2015, who is now the leader of the SLFP, and the Manifesto of the UNP at the parliamentary elections on 17 August 2015. The origins of the people's mandate for a New Constitution could even be traced back to the 1994 presidential elections, and subsequent presidential and parliamentary elections.

(This was part of a series of popular articles published in the *Colombo Telegraph, The Island* newspaper and the *Sri Lanka Guardian* in January 2016)

4

Strengthening Horizontal Democracy

"Can democracy be adequately understood in terms of majoritarian procedures?" - S. L. Hurley

The move for making a New Constitution has opened up considerable opportunities to deepen democracy in the country, and the indications so far reveal that vibrant discussions are taking place at present, among civil society organizations and political activists, sponsored by the Public Representation Committee (PRC), on a range of issues dealing particularly with (1) the local government system, (2) the creation of possible village/local level organizations, and (3) on how to encourage people's participation in decision making processes, among other matters. To the credit of the PRC and the promoters of a New Constitution it should be stated that such broader discussions were not held, or could not be held, during the formulation of the First or the Second Republican Constitutions in 1972 and 1978, or the aborted draft constitution in 2000. Apart from the necessary constitutional requirement to have a national referendum to finally approve a New Constitution (Article 83), the nature of the political changes that took place last year (8 January and 17 August), and the democratic political forces behind them, seem to be the catalysts for what is going on in the form of broad political discussions.

This article argues that to deepen democracy in Sri Lanka, or any country for that matter, measures need to be taken both horizontally and vertically. If provincial councils could be the main mechanisms through which democracy could be expanded horizontally, local governments constitute the potential of strengthening democracy both horizontally and vertically.

The Concept

Horizontal democracy is conceptualized by political scientists and others in different ways at different times. It is usually considered as opposite or different to vertical democracy. 'Different' may be the case, but 'opposite' is an overstatement. There is no system completely vertical or completely horizontal. The right combination of both might be the best for any country. In the evolution or development of democracy, there is a natural requirement to move away from a single (top down or bottom up) vertical structure towards more and more horizontal structures and practices. Representative democracy requires multiple formations and institutions created on the spatial scale. In the case of Sri Lanka, the provincial councils and local governments are the main formal institutions of horizontal democracy and from time to time the organizations or concepts such as 'Gramodaya Mandala' (village awakening councils), 'Jana Sabha' (people's councils) and now 'Grama Sabha' have been mooted for the same purposes.

Vertical versus horizontal modularity in political science is largely analogous to the same debates in cognitive science (about the mind and its processes) as S. L. Hurley initially explained in 1999, writing to the "Journal of Political Philosophy." The full title of the article is "Rationality, democracy and leaky boundaries: Vertical vs. horizontal modularity," for the benefit of anyone interested in reading. For a long time, there was a strong belief that 'rationality of mind' is a product of vertical cognition. Likewise political philosophers believed that the only rational system of democracy is a vertically designed single structure of democracy. The British Utilitarianism (i.e. Jeremy Bentham) was a high point in this belief in political philosophy.

In an extreme version of this belief, even 'checks and balances' were rejected or discarded as irrational. In the case of Sri Lanka, the strongest reflection of this vertical thinking was embodied in the 1972 Constitution, and then continued in the 1978, until the 13th Amendment came in. In the 1972 Constitution, checks and balances were minimized and unicameral legislature with the concept of 'supremacy of parliament' was instituted. It was a unitary state par excellence. It was also the opposite of liberal constitutionalism. In modern cognitive science, however, rationality of mind is not considered purely based on vertical modularity. It can depend on horizontal modularity as well. People may depend on lateral or parallel ways of reasoning to arrive at rational decisions and solutions to problems that they encounter. The concept of 'lateral thinking' developed by Edward de Bono has been a recognition of this understanding. It allows people to think 'out of the box' in finding solutions to their seemingly intractable problems.

In the same manner, there is the possibility of designing political structures to address complex social, economic, cultural and political problems through lateral or horizontal institutions. This means that within an overall 'pyramid,' installing smaller pyramids to countervail the authoritarian tendencies of otherwise a centralized structure. Any representative democracy takes the form of a pyramid. However, the smaller pyramids are much closer to the people; to their needs and aspirations. This has always been the case in history, although the strict Westphalian form of the state in the past period has kept a tight lid on the possibility until recently.

Some Roots

In political practice, the existence of horizontal structures or demand for them has always been the case even before the advent of modern democracy. The ancient political systems in many Asian countries including Sri Lanka were systems of *'Mandala,'* which consisted of a *'Manda'* (a Centre) and a *'La'* (a Periphery). The *'La'* was equally important as the *'Manda.'* *'Panchayath'* in India, and *'Gam Sabha'* (village councils) in Sri Lanka were the local varieties under this system. During the English revolutions in the 17th century, there were strong demands for horizontal democracy. 'Levelers' and 'Diggers' were the main advocates of these demands. Thereafter, the 'Chartists' carried forward these demands into the 19th century. The development of British 'County Councils' was greatly shaped by these movements and in turn influenced the local government system installed in Sri Lanka. What can be seen in the present system in Sri Lanka is the congruence between the ancient tradition and the British influence.

There were radical roots for the demand for more grassroots forms of horizontal democracy. Apart from the emergence of spontaneous people's councils in the American, the French or the Russian revolutions, Hannah Ardent has conceptualized a 'council system' based particularly on the experiences of the democracy movements that emerged in the Eastern European countries against totalitarianism. She first developed the idea in *"The Origins of Totalitarianism"* (1958 edition) and then elaborated the concept in her *"On Revolution"* (1963), particularly in the last chapter. This is what she said initially.

"In Hungary, we have seen the simultaneous setting-up of all kinds of councils, each of them corresponding to a previous existing group in which people habitually lived together or met regularly and knew each other. Thus the neighborhood councils emerged from sheer living together and grew into county and other territorial councils...."

Leslie Goonewardene of the LSSP was one who advocated such structures for Sri Lanka particularly in the late 1970s (i.e. "*A New Road is Needed*"). There were/are more militant (or extremist) versions of the thinking however. In recent times in the international arena, the term 'horizontal democracy' has surfaced in another meaning, more of political than institutional. It has been a popular slogan in the recent waves of democratic uprisings in the Middle East and North Africa (the 'Arab Springs'). For example, a leader of the Tunisian uprising, Yassine Brahim (now a Minister), had said "We don't need a charismatic leader. This is horizontal democracy. We are going to leverage social media to build horizontal democracy rather than a vertical democracy." According to him, the social media is supposedly playing a role in horizontal democracy movements. This sentiment has again and again resonated in other countries which took to the path of democratization or chaos. It could only be understood as reactive to a situation where the existing system was highly centralized and strictly vertical. Thus a more moderate view on horizontal democracy is necessary in my opinion.

Useful Principles

There are two main principles which are usually discussed and/or used in strengthening horizontal democracy. The first is devolution of power which we are familiar with. This means the relocation or transfer of (some) powers to a second tier of governmental institutions through the constitution. It can also go to a third tier. Depending on the amount of power allocation, degree of financial independence and more importantly the constitutional safeguards, the devolution of power can come closer even to federalism. The second is the principle of subsidiarity which we are not very familiar with or often misunderstood. In its pure form, this is a radical principle which gives primacy to the lowest level of governing institutions i.e. local government. Tocqueville's saying "the force of free people resides in the municipality" is often quoted as its explication. The principle says that 'whatever the local government can handle should be left with the local government system.' And only the rest should go to the provinces, and so on. It may be true that within a context of constitutional making in Sri Lanka, at present, the subsidiarity principle might not be practical in its full sense. However, it can be kept in mind (or used) both in allocating powers to the provincial councils and local government institutions, however realistically assessing their capacities and other consequences.

(Apart from the *Colombo Telegraph* and the *Sri Lanka Guardian*, *The Island* newspaper gave publicity to this article in February 2016)

5
Promoting Local Governance

"The force of free people resides in the municipality" - Alexis de Tocqueville

In today's politics, people usually look up to their leaders, representatives and the centers of power for solutions. As we have seen in the first part of this article ("Constitution Making and Strengthening Horizontal Democracy"), this thinking ruptures during progressive revolutionary upheavals or movements. However, this has not really been the case in Sri Lanka. For example, the leaders of the two rebellions or insurgencies, the JVP and the LTTE, in the South and in the North, wanted to create similar vertical structures instead of moving in the direction of more democratic horizontal structures. The political structures that the LTTE created were one good example. It is not clear yet, whether the incipient democracy movements that emerged last year are going in a different or the right direction. I am also not clear whether they are already dead or not!

New Ways

There are, however, new ways of communities and people looking at themselves and working together in finding solutions to their problems without necessarily neglecting or rejecting the usefulness of the vertical structures that are existing. I am in fact proposing a Middle Path. It is in this context that the importance of the local government system is important to our discussion. To reiterate, horizontal democracy and vertical democracy are not diametrically opposed to each other. Even in respect of local governance, there are strong elements of vertical structures which can be reformed and changed. Moreover, they are much closer to the people. To give a 'quantified' example, the distance between the people and Parliament in Sri Lanka is more than '300 times higher' than the distance between the people and a local council. There is one parliament, but 336 local councils. It may be a crude calculation, but the essence nevertheless is true. But in respect of capacity or power, the difference is quite the opposite given the existing legislation. This is why both horizontal and vertical structures are important in democracy and why horizontal structures should be strengthened with necessary capacity and 'power.'

After the next elections there will be 336 (not 335) local government bodies for approximately a 21 million population in Sri Lanka which is not a bad count by any means, as an average. Among them, 272 will be divisional councils *('Pradeshiya Sabhas')*, 40 urban councils and 24 municipalities. There is a new addition of Millaniya PS in the Kalutara district. One may even argue that the number can be reduced in the future, if the efficiency is increased, while strengthening the internal democratic structures. In Australia, there are only 565 councils to that massive size of the country, although the population is 23 million.

There is an obvious underestimation of urbanization in Sri Lanka with only 64 urban and municipal councils, and thus not delivering proper services to those populations within the present structure. In the Kalutara district, for example, there is no municipal council and only 4 urban councils. At present, the urbanization is calculated on the basis of the population in the urban and municipal council areas and not the other way round. The program for Megapolis might rectify this imbalance in the Western province, but probably getting the wrong end of the stick. There should always be a balance between 'democracy and efficiency' in all these type of reforms or otherwise one betrays the other. There are four districts, Polonnaruwa, Moneragala, Kilinochchi and Mullativu with only *'Pradeshiya Sabhas.'* The situation of latter two districts may be understandable due to the war situation in the past. But the situation in the former two districts, among other factors, signify some serious planning defects in respect of the present local government system.

Importance of LGs

The importance of the local government system is undeniable for democracy. When it is stifled, in a country like Sri Lanka, insurgency may erupt. There is one good example from our recent history. The withholding of elections to these councils between 1977 and 1988 was a major 'root cause' (though not the only one) of the insurrection that erupted in the North East in the form of separatist terrorist movement and that movement again prevented the holding of elections in those areas between 1994 and 2011. This is a lesson even for today not to postpone the local government elections unnecessarily. The opposition to *"Yahapalanaya"* might erupt from that source as some indications are already visible.

There were other defects of the local government system impinging on the democratic system or even the ethnic conflict in the country. Before the 13th Amendment, the system came under the control of the Minister in Colombo. The grievance on the part of the North was that the Minister favored the local councils in the South, neglecting the North and the East. Real or perceived, the accusation highlighted the importance of equal opportunity and equal treatment principles. The distances also mattered combined with language issues. This problem now is largely settled as the local government system is placed under the Provincial Councils. However, this imbalance may again arise within provinces (i.e. Eastern) if proper democratic structures and practices are not in place. Democracy is also not an abstract concept. Even people can become disgruntled about democracy, if the democratic institutions or structures cannot deliver necessary services and benefits to the people. This is a simple truth. When one looks at the purposes of the local government system, the tasks are impressive and closely relevant to the people's lives and needs. The potential is enormous.

The functions of the local government include as they stand (1) health and sanitation (2) construction and maintenance of local roads (3) housing and matters related to housing (4) public markets, parks, libraries, and (5) other utility services to the citizens. All these matters are listed under the objective of the "promotion of the comfort, convenience, and the welfare of the people." Even 'community development' is added to the list in respect of the *'Pradeshiya Sabhas'* since 1987. If these tasks are properly addressed, and the functions are faithfully performed, even employment could be generated and people's livelihood needs enhanced. Of course the functions and powers differ from the *'Predeshiya Sabhas'* to the urban councils or urban councils to the municipal councils. However, the above could be considered the main contours of the system.

The government has now published the demarcation of 4,834 wards applicable to the forthcoming LG elections. This is for 336 LG bodies with 4,583 single member and 251 multimember wards. It is not yet clear, however, whether the elections would be held only on the ward basis (under FPP) or a proportional representation also would be calculated above it as prescribed in the Local Government Elections Act as amended in 2012. The government gazette indicates the total of 5,099 members to be elected for 336 bodies. This is already an increase from the present number of 4,486. If the gazette has determined (as it appears) the number of council members, as the breakdowns have given for each and every LG body, then the PR calculation would be simply redundant.

This might vindicate what I have argued since 1999 (*"A New Electoral System for Sri Lanka?"*), that there is no much point in having a complicated PR system for local government elections, let alone the disastrous preferential voting. Newly demarcated 251 multimember seats could take care of some of the concerns that prompted a PR system at the local level. At local government elections, the priority should be for the selection of the best performing candidates and not necessarily the political parties.

Some Proposals

1. There are considerable opportunities even within the existing system to enhance people's participation that some of the civil society organizations are apparently talking about. It is announced that the next local government elections would be held under the Ward system. This is an opportunity to form and strengthen the Ward based people's or citizens' committees and organizations. This would be an enhancement of horizontal democracy. What might be possible is to form Ward Committees of the Citizens including the elected member or members, all contested candidates and representatives of the civil society organizations to look after the interests of the people in each and every ward of the relevant LG body.

2. As the two main political parties that are going to contest the LG elections, the UNP and the SLFP, are also in the same 'Yahapalana' government, the main competition or the selection should be about the best or the better candidate/s and not merely about the best party or the policies. At the local level, there is no much point in having 'deadly' party competitions. No one is going to rule the country by getting elected to a local council. Their task is to deliver the services to the people and the community.

3. There is a pressing need to resurrect the 'committee system' of governance, particularly in the local government system. The excessive powers of the Chairmen should be checked with the objective of abolishing them in the future. In the case of 'Pradeshiya Sabhas' already there is provision for appointing committees even with the participation of the citizens in the community (Section 12 of the Act). They can be on (a) finance and policy making (b) housing and community development (c) technical services and (d) environment and amenities. These are not formed or functioning. These should be implemented.

4. There is a clear prohibition of members or officers having direct or indirect financial interest in contracts or works of the 'Pradeshiya Sabhas.' It

is a punishable offense although clearly violated in practice (Section 219 of the Act). This provision should be fully implemented.

5. Most importantly, the local government system should be enshrined in the New Constitution. At present it is 'enshrined' or rather mentioned by default with the 13th Amendment as a devolved power. While this should be the case even in the future, there can be a Chapter on Local Governance emphasizing its importance, functions and revised structure/s with more accountability, efficiency and people's participation.

(The original of this article was published in *The Island* newspaper, the *Colombo Telegraph* and the *Sri Lanka Guardian* in February 2016)

Laksiri Fernando

6
Sri Lanka is Already 'Quasi Unitary'

"What's in a name? That which we call a rose by any other name would smell as sweet." - William Shakespeare

There are possibilities that the debates on the new constitution making process becoming polarized on 'unitary' versus 'federal' lines. This is unfortunate because the 'old distinctions' between the two do not exist any longer. The distinctions or differences are within a broad spectrum of state or constitutional types, and not between the above binary categories. It is only at the two extreme points that 'pure unitary' or 'pure federal' states may exist, and even that only in theory, but not in practice. Even in the case of Sri Lanka what exists is a 'quasi unitary' system and not an old type of 'unitary state' or a 'unitary constitution.' This became abundantly clear during the decision of the Supreme Court on the 13th Amendment. When the Amendment as a Bill was referred to the Supreme Court, a full bench of nine judges sat in judgement, and only five determined that it was not in contravention of the 'unitary state.' The opinion/s of the other four differed and they dissented.

Supreme Court Decision

Of course one can argue that the divisions/opinions of the judges were not purely on constitutional or legal grounds, judging from many ('political') judgements during and after that period. However, considering the main arguments of the petitioners, it is clear that the two main issues were about the 'unitary character of the state' and the 'supremacy of Parliament,' and therefore, the divided opinion reflects the ambiguity of these matters when the 13th Amendment was introduced. Let me quote the Supreme Court (majority) determination.

The Unitary character of the State of which the characteristics are the supremacy of the Central Parliament and the absence of subsidiary sovereign bodies remains unaffected. The Provincial Councils do not exercise sovereign legislative power and are only subsidiary bodies exercising limited legislative power subordinate to that of Parliament. Parliament has not thereby abdicated or in any manner alienated its legislative power in favour of any newly created legislative authority. The concept of devolution is used to mean the delegation of Central Government power without the relinquishment of supremacy. Devolution may be legislative or administrative or both and should be distinguished from decentralization. The scheme of devolution set out in the Bills does not erode the sovereignty of the People and does not require the approval of the People at a Referendum.

The majority view had taken the 'supremacy of the central parliament' and the 'absence of subsidiary (yet) sovereign bodies' as the main characteristics of a unitary state. To that extent they were correct in concluding that the 'unitary character of the state remains unaffected.' There is 'further extent' that they have not spelled out. That is that the provincial councils derive their authority also from the Constitution like the central Parliament. It is true that the provincial council system has not 'altered' the unitary character of the state, but 'qualified' it. It is not mere unitary state that exist now, but 'unitary state with devolution' or with extensive devolution. That was the intention of the 13th Amendment, emulating the Indian system, although it has not been done harmoniously. That is why changes with clear clarifications are necessary in a New Constitution. The 13th Amendment has not gone to the extent of federalism or even quasi federalism. It remains as, one could say, 'quasi unitary state.'

International Trends

How could we understand or interpret this quite a complex situation within the evolution of sates or constitutional systems in the world? When political scientists or constitutional lawyers defined 'unitary' or 'federal' states in early 20th century, there were only a limited number of states which were in existence. Others were vastly colonial territories. There was another category called 'confederations.' When the UN was formed in 1945, for example, there were only 51 member states but now 193 states. All these new states have written constitutions. Are they 'unitary' or 'federal'? The demarcations are quite mixed except in few cases. Even the old states have evolved in mixed directions. The UK, Spain, France and even the US have become complex combinations. The former Soviet Union was always a strange animal (with an authoritarian underbelly) and difficult to strictly categorize into any of the above three: 'confederal,' 'federal' or 'unitary.' Even China today shows mixed characteristics.

Let me quote briefly from three sources, first theoretical, second case-study, and third comparative analysis, to explain the current thinking on the subject.

States no longer feel that they have to make an exclusive choice between either unitary or federal systems. They sometimes devise hybrid combinations.

The above is stated in the *'Introduction to Politics'* by Robert Garner, Peter Ferdinand and Stephanie Lawson (Oxford University Press, 2012, p. 193). Even when Duncan Watts was trying to analyse government and politics in the US and UK which were traditionally called 'federal' and 'unitary' respectively (*Understanding US/UK Government and Politics*, Manchester University Press, 2003, p. 169), he said the following.

It is important not to emphasise unduly the formal differences between unitary and federal systems, for in practice the distinctions are less clear cut than at first appears.

Most important perhaps are the conclusions arrived at by analysing quite a number of countries and theories, and one of the contributors (John Loughlin) highlighting three salient points of the contemporary nation-states (Daniele Caramani, Ed., *Comparative Politics*, Oxford, 2014, p. 182).

The nation-state is the quintessentially modern form of political organization with distinctive features of territorial organization.

Claims that it is disappearing have been exaggerated.

The classical distinction between 'federal' and 'unitary' state is giving way to more complex forms of the nation-state.

Catuskoti Reasoning

It is possible for some people to reject the above conclusions or observations as Western theories. On the contrary, the Buddhist concept of *Catuskoti* is more helpful in understanding the evolving complexities of the nation-state than the binary debates on 'unitary vs. federal' theories. As Nyanaponika Thera explained (*The Heat of Meditation and Other Writings*, 2008, p. 74):

Today with the discovery of many-valued logic and the consequent realization that Aristotelian logic is only one of many possible systems, the significance of this Buddhist logic of four alternatives (catuskoti) could be better understood. Briefly, this is a two-valued logic of four alternatives unlike Aristotelian logic, which is a two-valued logic of two alternatives.

What does this mean in respect of what we are talking about as the nature of the states or constitutions? It means that 'black and white' distinctions between 'unitary and federal' are obsolete, or mistaken from the beginning. The reality is more complex. If I may translate one of Nyanaponika Thera's examples into our political problem: 'according to the Aristotelian (or formal) logic or reasoning, if a constitutional system is not unitary it is federal.' However, 'according to *catuskoti*, or four alternative reasoning (1) it can be unitary in main dimensions (2) it can be federal in the same manner, or (3) it can also be unitary in some dimensions but federal in other dimensions or (4) the state can be neither unitary nor federal. It is also clear from this reasoning that there can even be several other combinations in between. Dialectical reasoning also leads us to the same conclusions, going beyond the simplistic arguments or binary reasoning about 'unitary vs. federal' debate.

Conclusion

Our empirical evidence show, although I have not exhausted all, that with the 13th Amendment, our state system has transformed relatively into a new form. The Supreme Court's majority determination also noted that 'devolution should be distinguished from decentralization.' Decentralization is primarily a device in a unitary state, but devolution moves beyond its parameters. It was an understatement for the SC however to say that 'devolution may be legislative or administrative.' More correct is to say 'legislative or executive or both.' What the SC did not particularly spell out was the fact that provincial councils also derive their powers and legitimacy from the Constitution, without altering the supremacy of Parliament. Parliament retains the powers to legislate on national policies and the provincial councils are obliged to follow. In a small and a developing country like Sri Lanka this overarching policy determination is important through consensus and agreements. Cooperate devolution similar to cooperate federalism might be the best.

It is well known that devolution in Sri Lanka was intended to be modeled on the basis of the Indian system which is called 'quasi federalism.' However, this attempt was not a complete success under the presidential system, and for other reasons. India is not Unitary but a Union. Sri Lanka has not gone to that extent. Sri Lanka has retained its character as 'unitary' at least nominally and some people seems to be obsessed with this characterization. The present Article 2 says: *"The Republic of Sri Lanka is a Unitary State."* But more correct is to say: *The Republic of Sri Lanka is a Unitary State with Extensive Devolution.*

(This article was published in the *Colombo Telegraph*, *The Island* newspaper and the *Sri Lanka Guardian* in January 2016)

Laksiri Fernando

7
Federalism, Confederation or Separate State?

"Federalism is no longer the fault line of Centre-State relations but the definition of new partnership of Team India." - Narendra Modi

There is nothing wrong in proposing a viable federal system to Sri Lanka given the conflict context and its necessary resolution, in the short, the medium or the long term. In fact it is a must, unless it is stalled by adventurism. This means going beyond the existing devolution arrangements, already quasi-unitary in character. There can be other merits in expanding devolution towards a federal or a quasi-federal system, particularly taking the existing provinces as economic planning units, although Sri Lanka is a small country. The size of the country also should be taken into account, even though the population is nearly 21 million with three main ethnic or national communities are in competition or conflict. The other diversities should be taken into account not necessarily through the state structures but state practices and policies such as human rights, equal opportunities and political culture. What most suitable might be 'cooperative devolution' with constitutional safeguards to ensure that the center does not take back or infringe the powers and functions of the provinces, while coming closer to federalism or quasi-federalism.

NPC Proposals

It is unfortunate in this context what is proposed by the Northern Provincial Council (NPC) in April 2016 based on a draft prepared by the Tamil People's Council (TPC).[87] It is far far beyond the realistic conditions in the country and it cannot even be considered an ideal model. There is nothing particularly wrong in ideals, but they in that case should be impartial and open-minded. This quality is not there in the proposals. It is understandable that the proposals are from the Tamil side, or (major) part of the Tamil side. However, any reasonable proposal should be able to see the 'other' side, or the problems in a total Sri Lankan context.

One positive aspect of the proposals however is their clarity. Objectives are articulated clearly, and the proposed constitutional principles and structures are elaborated with details. Therefore it is necessary to assess them objectively without emotional outbursts. This is a responsibility on the part of all political parties and all concerned people. It is reported that a resolution based on the TPC draft is now handed over to the Speaker, Karu Jayasuriya, who is also the Chair of the recently constituted Constituent Assembly of Parliament, by the NPC Chief Minister, C. V. Wigneswaran. This is now official. What is not clear is the origin or the authorship of the proposals. Of course some of the ideas were there for a long time going beyond federalism, but I am here referring to the 'political authority' behind the proposals. Although the proposals are popularly named as TNA proposals, the text of the proposals are in the name of the Tamil People's Council. The exact title of the document says "Tamil People's Council: Final Proposals for Finding a Political Solution to the Tamil National Question."

The document is not something formulated by the TNA, or even the NPC, although the NPC Chief Minister was apparently involved in the process and there had undoubtedly been many public consultations before its final formulation. What the NPC has done apparently is to pass the proposals through a resolution on 22 April 2016 with 28 members sitting and 10 absent. According to the website of the TPC, a sub-committee was appointed to formulate the proposals on 2 January 2016 and an initial proposal was inaugurated on 31 January within a month for public consultations. We have to keep in mind that the founding of the TPC was

---

[87] Asian Mirror published the full text on 24 April 2016. http://www.asianmirror.lk/news/item/16130-northern-provincial-council-resolution-full-text

only on 19 December 2015. According to the same website, there had been a five member external panel assisting the proposals, and as it says, including "two foreign experts on constitution and three experts from Diaspora." The names are not given. None of the above should discount the seriousness of the proposals or their necessary critical evaluation in the process of finding a constitutional framework for a viable solution to the ethnic confrontations in the country. However it appears that the proposals are more political or ideological than constitutional as will be discussed below.

Framework

The proposals constitute two clear parts (1) a very long Preamble expressing political or ideological objectives and (2) constitutional proposals which calls for a loose confederation with a weak 'federal' or 'central' government. In this 6,912 word document, 1,916 words are spent on the Preamble and the call for a 'political agreement prior to a constitutional enactment.' It is intriguing to contemplate why this size of a preamble was required if the purpose is for a 'political agreement' and a subsequent 'constitutional enactment.'

The Preamble can be extremely controversial and might be counterproductive for any pragmatic solution/s that could be achieved based on some of the proposals in the section on the constitution. It begins by saying "*throughout the centuries from the dawn of history, the Sinhalese and Tamil nations have divided between themselves the possession of Ceylon.*" Even if we leave out the historical inaccuracy of the first part in respect of the origins of the 'nations,' it is questionable why the claims of the Sinhalese and the Tamils are considered as a matter of 'dividing the possessions of the country, between the two groups.' Are we talking about a conflict for 'real-estate' or material possessions? If that is the case, the ordinary people are not part of it, except they are mobilized on emotional grounds.

It may be correct to consider the Kings and their families divided the possessions of the country between themselves in old days (with some corollaries in recent times), but not the people. Even that not necessarily on ethnic or nation lines but on the basis of dynasties. The first three paragraphs delightfully talk about the ancient Kingdoms. It may be the case that the drafters wanted to trace the history. But the way that has been done gives the impression that at least the first approach of the proposal is quite primordial. The primordial approach in nationalism is quite well known. As the "The Nationalism Project" rather critically says, "*Nationalists argue that nations are timeless phenomena. When man climbed out of the primordial slime, he immediately set about creating nations.*"[88] This primordial approach is shared by both the Sinhalese and the Tamil extremists. At least they have one point in agreement!

Ideological Approach

The above does not mean that the whole historical narrative traced in the Preamble, particularly for the period after independence is completely incorrect. There is a general agreement among the moderate people about some of the points traced in the paragraph seven which begins by saying, *"Acknowledging that successive Sinhalese governments since independence have always* [sic] *encouraged and fostered the aggressive nationalism of the Sinhalese people and have used their political power to the detriment of the Tamils,"* irrespective of the explosive language used and exaggerations or distortions committed.

However, it is questionable whether this is the way to go about political negotiations for a constitutional settlement for the national question. It is strange again to note the reference to the 'territories of the former Tamil Kingdom' when it refers to 'a system of planned state-organized Sinhalese colonization' in point (b) in the same paragraph. Be as it may, more controversial might be the assertion of the Vaddukoddai resolution (1976) and the Thimpu principles (1985) as a Preamble to constitutional negotiations. Nowhere in the proposal is it said that the TPC is not asking for a separate state, although this has been repeated by some of the TNA leaders. Instead, the catastrophic adventure of the LTTE is defended in the following terms.

Bearing in mind that the Tamil armed struggle as a measure of self-defense and as a means for the realization of the Tamil rights to self-determination arose only after more than four decades of non-violent and peaceful constitutional struggle / attempts by the various Tamil political parties to win their rights, by co-operating with the successive governments in order to achieve the bare minimum of political rights proved to be futile and due to the absence of means to resolve the conflict peacefully.

It is a subjective or unilateral assessment to say about the complete exhaustion of 'more than four decades of non-violent and peaceful constitutional struggle/attempts' - while there is some relative truth in it. What we have to understand is that the struggle for democracy is a long and an arduous struggle. (By the way I have not seen the concept of democracy

---

[88] See The Nationalism Project by Eric G. E. Zuelow http://www.nationalismproject.org/

or the word 'democracy' appearing in any significant manner in the whole document.) There are various forms of 'non-violent and peaceful struggles.' If there is no engagement or dialogue, then those might not reap results. However, none of those would justify the so-called "Tamil armed struggle as a measure of self-defense" or "as a means for the realization of the Tamil rights for self-determination." In my view, the statement is a clear justification of LTTE terrorism which is unfortunate and unacceptable.

Constitutional Structure?

It may be true that the proposal has not directly called for a 'separation of the country.' But it has called for a weak Federation and strong (provincial) States, North-East as a Tamil state. For example, the document proposes 55 powers for the States, but 37 powers for the Federation! The interpretation of these powers and the 'mix' of the 'federation and the states' are as follows. Let me quote the full section to give a taste of it. This is titled "Powers of the Federation and the States" (Section 8).

8.1. Powers of Government shall be shared between the Federation (Centre) and the States.

8.2. The Federal List of the Constitution shall determine the powers to be exercised by the Federation.

8.3. The States shall exercise all powers not falling within the Federal List including those powers listed under the States List.

8.4. The Federation and the States shall be supreme in their respective spheres of competence.

The 'fashionable' proposition (yet erroneous or ambiguous from the beginning in my opinion) for 'power-sharing' seems to be the formula that was utilized for the 'mingled' arrangement. Thus it proposes to share power 'between the Federation (Centre) and the States' particularly between the 'Centre and the (Tamil) North-East State.' There is an interesting 'Note' to the section that I have quoted above, which says *"The States' List has been prepared from the perspective of the powers that the North-East State Assembly would exercise."* This is in a way understandable, because it talks about 'Tamil' interests or aspirations. What the proposal has perceived is a multi-unit federation and question whether there is a need to have the same powers for the 'other units' saying, *"We recognize that unlike the North-East no other part of the country makes claims to maximum self-government."*

Most intriguing are the last two sub-sections (8.3 and 8.4) which says (1) 'the States (read North-East) shall exercise *all powers* not falling within the Federal List' and (2) 'the Federation and the States (again read North-East) shall be *supreme* in their respective spheres.' This is about a 'separate state' within a loose federation, with 'supremacy for that state' in its own sphere.

(This article was published in the *Colombo Telegraph*, *The Island* and the *Sri Lanka Guardian* in April 2016)

8
Going Beyond the 13-A and Towards Cooperative Devolution

Discussions have started on devolution and/or federalism in the context of constitutional reforms and the present is an attempt to clarify some of the important issues in the form of 'questions and answers.' The purpose is to deviate from abstract debates and bring concreate substance to the discussions as far as I can contribute, in the form of a series of relevant questions and answers.

Question: What is meant by 'going beyond the 13th Amendment'?
Answer: I basically mean four things. (1) Reducing the concurrent list (2) eliminating the ambiguities between the national list and the provincial list (3) reducing the powers of the Governor and (4) creating a framework for making sufficient fiscal and administrative resources available to the provinces.

Question: Why not completely replace devolution and go for federalism?
Answer: Devolution is part of federalism. There is no one form of federalism but different forms. As Shakespeare said, 'a rose by any other name would smell as sweet.' It is more appropriate to call the present or a future system devolution, given its history and the form. We are evolving from a unitary state towards a more federal structure. Our evolution is devolution.

Question: Why should anyone qualify devolution as cooperative devolution? What does it mean?

Answer: It is similar to cooperative federalism. When I was studying in Canada in the mid-1970s, the concept evolved there. There are many books written on the subject. Prime Minister Pierre Trudeau (not Justin) started to meet with the state Premiers to sort out matters. His particular interest was to appease the rebellious Quebec. It worked. Thereafter concreate mechanisms were devised for cooperation. In 1990/91 when the Australian Prime Minister Bob Hawke wanted to pursue a national economic reform agenda he started to meet with the state Premiers. It partially worked. This cooperation is a practice continued even today. It is called cooperative or collaborative federalism. There can be mechanisms for cooperation.

Question: But what is its relevance to Sri Lanka?

Answer: Take a recent most example. Due to the ongoing high heat in the North Central Province they have decided to close the schools at 12 noon. But the central government ministry continues to have the national schools open as usual. On this smallest thing they cannot cooperate. This has created confusion among the citizens. Not only that. The central ministry seems to dictate terms to the provincial ministry with an expert report! I am not saying whose view is correct. But wish to emphasize that there should be cooperation. The central government should not interfere. Provinces should also cooperate.

Question: The example can be just incidental, can't it?

Answer: No. There are so many examples. Take the controversy about building 65,000 houses in the north and the east for displaced people for resettlement. Some people say the scheme is too costly and steel houses are not suitable to the climate. I am not making a judgement on either. But what is apparent is that the central ministry has not consulted the provincial councils or the competent civil society organizations on the matter. The latter expressed concerns first, and then the provincial council jumped on the matter perhaps for political reasons.

This is what failed during the Rajapaksa regime. Northern provincial council elections were delayed. Through the Task Force, unilateral developments were undertaken perhaps some aspects not meeting the needs of the people. I am not discounting what was done. I think the Central Bank estimated that around US$ 3 billion was spent on resettlement, rehabilitation and development. That is great. But what is the point if the people are not satisfied. That is why cooperation is necessary for devolution and beyond. We have to move from coercive or unilateral devolution to cooperative devolution.

Question: It was mentioned that the concurrent list should be reduced. What do you mean and can an example be given?

Answer: For example, school education should completely be a devolved function in my opinion. All schools from pre-schools to GCE A/L should come under the provincial councils. It would be a relief for the central government and an empowerment for the provincial councils. At present 'national schools' are under the central government. Education also appears in the concurrent list as sections 3 and 4 apart from the provincial list. This is out of 36 items or sections. These two sections should be taken out. This is an example of reducing the concurrent list.

Why? The reason is that when a matter is in the concurrent list the central government can encroach easily. This is against the principle of autonomy. I am not talking about complete or absolute autonomy but relative or necessary autonomy.

The school education should be guided under national policies, bench marks and curricular. In formulating national policies on school education, there should be center-periphery cooperation. Both the GCE O/L and A/L can be conducted by an institution like the National Institute of Education (NIE). It is true that in a proper federal system even such examinations are conducted by the states. But here we are talking about 'devolution and provinces' and not proper 'federalism or states.' The size of the country, proximity between the center and periphery and the stage of economic and social development are also reasons to have uniform senior school examinations. Different examination systems would not be useful.

Question: Some people say that concurrent list should be completely eliminated? What do you say?

Answer: I don't subscribe to that view. You cannot surgically separate government functions completely into central functions and provincial functions. It is artificial. It is also against the spirit of cooperative devolution. However, one danger of a concurrent list is the tendency for a central government to take over the functions of that list. That should be prevented. That can be prevented in the constitution. Another preventive measure is the reduction of the concurrent list as I have suggested.

Another creative possibility is to have a 'cooperative list' instead or in addition to a concurrent list. To have in addition is a complicated matter because in a 'citizen friendly' constitution the matters should not be so complicated. Normally matters come under a concurrent list when they overlap. But to be more positive or proactive, those are also the areas that cooperation is most necessary. Therefore, naming concurrent matters under a cooperative list is more logical and positive.

Question: Some people also say the residual powers also should be with the provinces. What are the residual powers? And what do you say?

Answer: Residual power normally means what is not listed or unknown at the time of constitution making. It can also be a device to keep the listing to a minimum, declaring that the 'residual power' is with the center or the provinces. Traditionally, if the residual power is with the states that is called a 'full-federal' system and if the residual power is with the center it is called a 'semi-federal' system. That is one reason why India is called semi-federal. However, this is not always the case. In Canada, residual powers go to the center but it is federal and not semi.

In a system of devolution, it is understood that 'residual power' is with the center, because the powers are devolved from the center. In our present constitution 'all subjects and functions not specified in the provincial list or the concurrent list' come under the reserved list for the center.

Question: Is it that full federalism is premature for Sri Lanka?

Answer: Yes, in a way yes. We have to build upon what we have now. It is also political realism consonant with normative principles on the matter. We have actually not properly implemented what we have. One reason was the continuation of the war until it ended in 2009 with much controversy. The other still remaining reason is the political controversies surrounding even on devolution. The latter is partly due to the ambiguities existing in the present constitution. Although we call the change last year a 'revolution' it is not a revolution proper. It is so-called. We have to take an evolutionary path. That is the best, the safest and most practical. We should not fall back to an open conflict again.

We adopted the devolutionary model from India. It is akin to our ancient 'Manda-la' (center-periphery) system. Federalism, regional councils and then provincial councils were in our discussion agendas for a very long time. The Indian model is called semi or quasi-federal. 'Federalism,' 'unitary-state' or 'devolution' are all matters of degree. We should focus more on substance and purposes and not name boards. Let me quote Shakespeare again: 'a rose by any other name would smell as sweet.'

(This article was published in *The Island*, the *Colombo Telegraph* and the *Sri Lanka Guardian* in May 2016)

9
More Q&A on Devolution and Constitution Making

Addressing the question of devolution undoubtedly might be the most controversial among the constitutional issues facing Sri Lanka today. There are both 'pull and push' factors in operation dividing the people and political parties, on ethnic and other grounds. As a follow up to the previous article on *"Going Beyond the 13-A and Towards Cooperative Devolution"* (8 May 2016) this is a further attempt to address some of the other key issues in the form of 'questions and answers.' The purpose is to deviate from abstract debates and bring some concrete substance to the discussions. While the attempt is to be brief, objective and detached as much as possible, the answers admittedly constitute the author's personal opinions.

Question: What could be the 'nature of the state' in a new constitution? Is it possible not to write about it?
Answer: A constitution can be silent on the nature of the state. That can seemingly prevent a controversy. For example, the Soulbury constitution (1947) did not characterize the nature of the state. But it was a unitary state. We have to keep in mind however that the Soulbury constitution was not designed for full independence. For a fully-fledged independent constitution the characterization of the state is important. That is what happened in 1972.

There can be a delicate difference between what is written in a constitution and the actual nature of the state. This is our situation at present. Present constitution characterizes the state as unitary. But after devolution, under the 13th Amendment (1987), in fact the character is not strictly unitary, but quasi-unitary. The constitution also names the state as 'socialist.' But we are no near socialism. There is no point in keeping it any longer. We have a tradition of writing the constitution in a single document. There is no possibility of changing it. Writing the nature of the state is therefore almost unavoidable. The nature of the state however does not limit to the controversy over 'unitary vs. federal.' The nature of the state should be democratic. This is where we should pay more attention. Our society is also plural, multicultural and multi-religious. This should reflect in the constitution. That can address some of the controversial issues on ethnic and religious lines. It is best to incorporate the actual situation and actual interests.

Question: Is it possible then to avoid characterizing the state as unitary? What is the most realistic formulation?
Answer: There is a strong feeling that the unitary character of the state should be preserved. One reason is the experience of separatism. The enforcement of the unitary principle is considered as a guarantee to prevent separation. On the other hand, those who want to drop the unitary characterization feel that it allows the central government to interfere unnecessarily in provincial matters. Therefore, the best or the rational compromise might be to 'write the unitary character but qualify it.' For example, in could be written "Sri Lanka is a unitary state with devolution of power to the nine provinces as prescribed in the constitution." A 'devolved unitary state' is and might be the future situation.

Question: What is the rationale behind the demand or proposal to have the North-East as one province? What would be the implications as a result of it?
Answer: 'Ethno-federalism' seems to be the justification behind the demand or the proposal. However in Sri Lanka we are talking about devolution and not federalism proper. We are premature for federalism. Anyway, ethno-federalism is not a desirable system. In respect of devolution, there can be three types: (1) purely based on ethnic considerations (2) purely based on administrative/political considerations and (3) considering both ethnic and political/administrative factors. Sri Lanka is well suited for the third model and that is the best for democracy, development and ethnic harmony.

The existing nine provinces are conducive for a desirable balance. The Northern Province can take care of the interests of the SL Tamils also respecting the minorities within it. The Eastern Province can be an experiment or even exemplary in ethnic harmony between the Muslims, the Tamils and the Sinhalese. There can be a good balance. The Central Province also should take good care of the hill country Tamils and also the Muslims. The other provinces also should do the same. The overarching protection should be through the fundamental human rights and their protective mechanisms. If the provinces are going to be re-demarcated or united purely on perceived ethnic lines it would end up in a political mess probably leading to another civil war. Even from an aerial viewpoint, the North-East as one province is artificial.

Question: Are there research findings to support the advisability of 'neutrally demarcated' units in contrast to 'ethnically demarcated' ones in devolution or federalism?

Answer: Yes. Research observations on federalism on these lines are equally valid for devolution. For example, prior to the drafting of the post-apartheid democratic constitution of South Africa in 1996 there were extensive research conducted on the subject particularly by the Human Sciences Research Council. The following is what Professor Daniel Elazar said on this matter (*"Federalism Theory and Application"* Vol. 1, 1995, p. 17).

Federal systems have been more successful over the long run when there has been a healthy dose of the second, namely, the divisions of the overall population along neutral territorial lines so that whatever set of interests occupies a particular territory at a given time can find expression through the institutions of that territory, both locally and in the federal whole.

Even in South Africa there are exactly nine provinces. However, demarcations have not overtly followed an ethnic or language criteria. South Africa is also a unitary state with devolution. Switzerland has three main ethnic communities (German, French and Italian) and a smaller community (Romansh). However, there are 26 Cantons. This means cantons are not demarcated strictly on ethnic lines.

Question: Some people propose to make Sri Lanka a secular state. Is it desirable or necessary?

Answer: It could be desirable. Linking the state with a religion is not a good idea. Religion is a private matter. Perhaps Buddhism required state patronage in ancient times. It is not necessary today. The value and respect for Buddhism would increase if it is free from direct state patronage. The present article in the constitution on Buddhism (Article 9) however does not make Sri Lanka a Buddhist state. It gives foremost place to Buddhism while protecting other religions. Religious freedom is and can be protected under fundamental human rights and other means. It is admirable that India is a secular state. But whether it can be achieved completely in Sri Lanka at present is questionable. It would be better if Mahanayakes express a positive view on this matter. What might be possible at this stage is to balance the 'foremost place for Buddhism' with 'religious freedoms' and perhaps make the 'foremost place' more neutral. It is not good to have a major controversy on the subject.

Question: On the question of devolution, two contentious issues are police and land powers. Is it desirable to devolve police powers to the provinces? Would they be able to handle 'law and order' completely on their own?

Answer: It would be extremely difficult to handover full police powers to the provinces even if they are capable of handling them. What might be possible is to establish and handover 'community policing' to the provincial councils including 'traffic police.' This will be a relief for the national government and empowerment for the provinces. There should be however cooperation between the national police and the (provincial) community police and Sri Lanka already has some experiments in community policing.

At present, there is a pressing need for a comprehensive reform in the police service. Police reforms should be conducted nationally and not provincially. The necessary reforms should entail: (1) establishment of complete political independence (2) extensive legal training and professional high standards for all officers and (3) complete elimination of torture and inhuman practices, among other things. There is no much point in provincial councils asking for police powers. The ordinary people are not going to benefit. Instead, politicization might escalate under the provincial administration.

Question: Another contentious issue is land powers. Would the state-land be vested with the national government or the provincial councils? What are the best options in resolving the controversy?

Answer: This is undoubtedly an area where 'cooperative devolution' should apply. Land is one of the precious natural resources in Sri Lanka. As agriculture is (going to be) a devolved subject, provinces definitely should have some hold on land and even land settlement. Provinces should not depend on the center's mercy. Here we are talking about state or public land and not private land. Land is also necessary for other provincial functions such as 'community development' or 'housing.' What might be prevented is arbitrary land alienation by the provinces or the center. Strictly independent 'national land commission' might be the solution for this and other purposes.

Since Sri Lanka is a developing country and the distribution of public land is highly uneven between provinces there should be a national policy as well as an overall national responsibility. In respect of allocating (not dividing) public land between the center and the provinces, a percentage formula can apply. In determining an exact formula, proper research might be necessary. Land unfortunately is an under-researched area.

(This article was sequel to the previous article published in the same printed and web newspapers in May 2016)

10
Electoral Reforms Should Take Equal Priority

"The ballet is stronger than the bullet." - Abraham Lincoln

In February 2015, the 'National Executive Council' formed to strengthen democracy after the political change in January, brought out a 'Discussion Paper on Constitutional Reforms' without any outline for electoral reforms.[89] My observations on the discussion paper however will be outlined some other time but before that the importance of electoral reforms should be highlighted. My preliminary observation nevertheless is that it should have been titled or explained as 'interim measures' for the abolition of the presidential system. Without that clarity the proposals already have created some confusion or misgivings. It should be the case even in electoral reforms and they should be 'interim' to mean a New Constitution should be inaugurated preferably through a Constituent Assembly after a complete 'free and fair' general election.

Importance of Electoral Reforms

Even when one refer to the genesis of the presidential system proposed by J. R. Jayewardene initially in December 1966 before the "Ceylon Association for the Advancement of Science," he not only proposed to change the 'parliamentary executive system' which he disparaged as depended on "the whims and fancies of an elected legislature." He also proposed to change the electoral system which gave rise, according to him, to those 'whims and fancies,' "where the elector elects his legislator according to the defined electoral areas." (See *Selected Speeches 1944-1973*, pp. 89-93).

---

[89] For an outline of the paper see "The Discussion Paper on Constitutional Reforms in Sri Lanka," *Sri Lanka BRIEF*, 9 February 2015.

The logic of his two reforms depended on his argument or belief that (1) "Among the new emerging nations in the continents of Africa and Asia, only two countries, India and Ceylon, have preserved democratic system of Government," (2) "The politicians in power know what is wrong in the economy, they are aware of the remedy, but the desire to be popular and to secure a majority of votes at a general election prevents them from taking the correct remedial measures," and (3) "If then the system of democratic government has failed in some aspects, we should not hesitate to think of changes and amendments in that system where necessary." (Ibid).

Not only his 'theory,' but also the practice shows that the draconian presidential system in Sri Lanka was erected on a corrupt electoral system. Both systems worked towards one end and that is to undermine the democratic system and people's influence in the representative government. Therefore, there is no much point in changing one without the other. Both are two sides of the same coin. What is wrong in the electoral system is not the proportional representation per se, but the abolition of the 'small electorates' of 160 (single and multimember) seats previously existed where voters had some control or influence over the election of their Members of Parliament (MP) and their performance thereafter.

As a proper record of history it should however be noted that the present electoral system came into operation only after J. R. Jayewardene in 1989 and before that the manipulation or the control of the legislature was achieved directly through 'undated letters of resignation' from the MPs and the extension of the period of Parliament by the controversial referendum in 1982. Could the new generations of voters believe that there were no parliamentary elections between 1977 and 1989 for twelve years? That period was the (first) mother of all major conflicts and distortions of the democratic system in the country.

The Money Factor

There is much understanding about the adverse effects of the preferential vote competition which begets electoral violence and rivalry even within the same party or coalition not to speak of inter-party violence. The killing of Bharatha Lakshman in October 2011 was directly associated with this predicament, but only one instance. That is also not the only ailment. There were 160 electorates in 1977 but they became reduced to 22 in 1989. It is the same today. As the election competitions take place within a larger arena of a District, to be a viable contender of a party, a candidate in general requires a considerable amount of money of his own or from others. These are estimated to be in millions if not billions. This may be different in the case of political parties like the JVP, but I am talking in general terms. Even the well-established political parties (the SLFP or the UNP) are not in a position to undertake their candidates' major expenses. The natural result is the dependence of candidates or political parties on financiers and benefactors.

The system also effectively excludes the independent candidate. Independent candidates, depending on the choice of the people, play an important role in a proper representative system. Australia is one example. The most glaring in this system is the denial of the particular political right accorded in Article 25 (b) in the 'International Covenant on Civil and Political Rights' (ICCPR), to eligible everyone "to vote and to be elected at genuine periodic elections." In Sri Lanka, while all eligible may have the vote, all eligible who 'intends to be elected,' to mean to contest, cannot do so under the restrictive circumstances. There are no equal opportunities for those who may have necessary commitment and ideas but lack sufficient money or right (actually wrong!) contacts. Women are also largely debarred from the system because of violent competitions. There is no level playing field under the system.

To come back to the earlier point about political financers, these benefactors are not philanthropists. They expect a big price in return. They may also not be the formal business people or companies. They usually are the contractors or emerging business people who desperately require government patronage. The new entrants to this 'philanthropy' allegedly are the drug and the ethanol dealers. So far revealed information about 'Mr. Wele Sudha' indicates to one of these connections.[90] The same goes for the alleged involvement of a former Prime Minister and/or his son. The system had been so corrupt, even after the public revelations, the PM didn't have the decency to resign. The President looked on or acquiesced.

Let me relate a personal story. Somewhere in 2003, I was invited to meet with the then Leader of the Opposition (LO) to see whether I could academically assist him in his political work. The person who arranged the meeting was my name sake, a friend, an advisor to the LO. When the LO was late for the meeting and when I was naturally uneasy, my friend informed me that the LO was having lunch with some unknown business people who are the benefactors of his and also the party's election campaigns. I had to reluctantly understand the situation because otherwise under the prevailing system, one has to wait for a 'Tsunami of funds' to

---

[90] Wele Sudha was convicted for drug trafficking in October 2015 who apparently had political patronage.

come to conduct elections. That was exactly what happened in 2005.

The Presidential Factor

But lately there had appeared other ways as well. A wily president could entice even the opposition quite easily, under the circumstances, to cross over in order that he could manipulate and control the Parliament. The then Chief Justice bent the law to this effect. Otherwise, many 'Honorable Members of Parliament' could not payback the election financiers. Other than paying back the financiers, they themselves have to finance themselves, their boisterous sons, families and friends. That was natural or appeared 'normal' under the corrupt political culture created under the present electoral system. Politics became a big dirty business even with foreign connections and affiliations, not with the West as usually accused of, except in some Casino related cases, but with some countries and personalities in the East. In return they were given concessions in the Stock Market, Board of Investment (BOI) or in mega projects and contracts. These deals were considered 'culturally correct.'

The most distorted and undermined two cardinal principles of democracy as a result were: (1) the necessary representative link between the voters and the voted, and (2) the genuine party affiliations of politicians on public policy grounds. All became blurred and distorted. At the 2004 elections, the opposition was quite strong like in 1994 or 1999. After the presidential elections in 2005, it became weak, because 39 members crossed over to the government. By 2010 elections, the opposition was pathetically weak. Yet, 16 members again crossed over to the government. The payback could only be managed for the financiers or for themselves by being part of the government not merely as MPs but as Ministers. Therefore, Sri Lanka went into the Guinness Book with the largest Cabinet (65) in the world, and altogether having 105 Ministers in a 225 Parliament.[91]

Subsequent to all these corrupt achievements, it was no wonder that the most skillful operator after J. R. Jayewardene - Mahinda Rajapaksa - tried to perpetuate his and/or family power beyond the constitutional limitations even Jayewardene himself could not visualize, through the 18th Amendment as his next logical step. All these evolved parallel to and beyond the war against LTTE terrorism with or without a direct link between the two, except perhaps in the case of arms deals. During the period of the war,

---

[91] The present situation apparently is not different. As of April 2016, there were 47 members in the Cabinet (the President and the Prime Minister and 45 other Ministers) and 25 Deputy Ministers and 20 other State Ministers.

people or even the political analysts were not in a proper position to assess the complete gravity of the whole distortion or degeneration of the democratic system.

Conclusion

As I have outlined from the beginning, the root causes of this abuse of democracy, however, are not only within that of 'personality' or the 'presidential powers.' They are within the 'electoral system' as well. One cannot be separated from the other/s. One component of the corrupt political cycle at least temporarily taken away now. The vicious political cycle is temporarily broken, if I may say, thanks to the 'Astrologers of the 8th of January.'[92] The cycle would not be broken permanently, however, merely by changing the presidential powers. There is almost a natural propensity in politics to be corrupt. There should be strong checks and balances to counter them in any country. Unless the incorrigibly corrupt electoral system is changed, the new President or the new Prime Minister may also be forced to play the same role by gratifying his supporters through a larger Cabinet, additional ministerial positions and other benefits. Even the whole system might become blind again to corruption of the politicians and the officials.

What is most important is to create a healthy electoral system where (1) the elected are closer to the electors, (2) the elected or the MPs consider the position as a duty or service and not a privilege, and (3) civil society or citizens' associations are organized at the electoral level to be vigilant about their representatives. The above three principles may appear too ideal to some. But if those are taken as objectives, the present electoral system could be reformed even as an interim measure until a permanent system is elaborated with a New Constitution in the future. Unless some basic changes are made before the next parliamentary elections, the quality of the parliament will not be conducive for a national unity government or for democracy.

(This article was published in the *Colombo Telegraph* and the *Sri Lanka Guardian* in February 2016)

---

[92] It is believed that an Astrologer's advice precipitated the holding of the elections in January 2015, two years prior to its due in 2017.

PART II

PROPOSALS FOR A
NEW CONSTITUTION

SUBMISSIONS TO THE
PUBLIC REPRESENTATION COMMITTEE (RPC)
FEBRUARY 2016

Laksiri Fernando

11
Proposals for a New Constitution

The Public Representation Committee (PRC) appointed by the government to seek opinions from the public and to hold public consultations in different parts of the country, requested interested parties and citizens to submit written proposals on 20 topics outlined by its website. The present chapter consists of the proposals submitted by the present author on all those topics, in the given order, addressed to the Chairman of the PRC, Lal Wijenayake, on 3 March 2016, without any alteration or editing, except the formatting. It was also noted, in the covering letter to the Chairman that these proposals are made 'as an independent academic, based on study and experience and without any partisan political opinion or advancing any personal or group interest.' The following foreword is also as of the original.

Foreword

Discontinuity and continuity appear to be part and parcel of constitution making and constitutional evolution in many countries except where major revolutions occur. Where discontinuity is intended, 'innovation' should take its place. It is not good for any country to move from one extreme to the other. The best policy would be to strike a balance and follow a Middle Path. After all, good governance or democracy does not depend solely on the niceties of a constitution. Practice is more important than theory.

Constitutional making is particularly difficult in divided societies. An incrementalist approach might be the best. If I may borrow some ideas from Hanna Lerner, the following might be the best (*Making Constitutions in Deeply Divided Societies*, 2011):

Avoidance of controversial formulations or change, the use of neutral legal language, and inclusion of contrasting provisions, yet absolute clarity in operational articles.

A good constitution can compromise in its visionary formulations, yet unambiguous in operational principles. The use of plain language also has become the norm of 'people-centered constitution making' in many countries. It is in the above spirit and principles that the following proposals are made for the proposed New Constitution. Proposals are not necessarily my personal views or ideals. They are a compromise between 'what is desirable' and 'what is feasible.' However, fundamental democratic principles are not compromised. It should be noted that when clear formulations are proposed those are *italicized*. Other proposals are in ordinary font. Rationale for the proposals are given only when they are necessary.

1. Nature of the State

Proposal:

Sri Lanka (Ceylon) is a Free, Sovereign, Independent, Indissoluble, Plural and Democratic Republic and shall be known as the Republic of Sri Lanka.

The Republic of Sri Lanka is a Unitary State with Devolution of Power in Nine Provinces as prescribed in this Constitution. The State takes responsibility for peace, unity and welfare of the people. The State shall preserve and advance a Sri Lankan identity while recognizing multi-ethnic, multi-lingual, multi-religious and multi-cultural character of the Sri Lankan society.

In the Republic of Sri Lanka sovereignty is in the people and is inalienable. Sovereignty includes the powers of government at national, provincial and local levels, fundamental human rights and the franchise. The sovereignty is exercised through representative institutions while the people retaining the ultimate authority.

Rationale:

In describing the Nature of the State, both the 1972 and 1978 constitutions use the terms 'free,' 'sovereign,' 'independent' and 'democratic.' In addition, this proposal uses the terms 'indissoluble' and 'plural' in that order. It is a compromise formulation to emphasize the 'plural' character within an 'indissoluble' state. In the proposer's personal opinion, the State also shall be 'secular' and 'federal.' However, it is not proposed. There can be alternative ways of coming closer to both objectives and particularly for a 'secular' state through various other provisions of the constitution i.e. fundamental human rights, chapter on religion, independence of the judiciary, rule of law and ensuring independent and impartial public service.

It might be practically impossible to change the present formulation 'Sri Lanka as a unitary state.' Instead, a compromise is proposed to include devolution of power in the same sentence as a qualification. What is proposed promoting Sri Lankan identity while recognizing multi-ethnic, multi-religious, multi-lingual and multi-cultural character of the Sri Lankan society is very much similar to the August 2000 draft. However, the present proposal has given priority to multi-religious character after stating multi-ethnic character. This is necessary recognizing the Muslim or other religious identities.

The description of peoples' sovereignty is elaborated. 'The powers of the government' as part of sovereignty are defined to include the 'powers at the center, the provinces and the local governments.' This is an implied recognition of 'shared sovereignty' not purely in ethnic terms but in horizontal dimensions. A fundamental difference is the inclusion of the following sentence as a clarification of people's sovereignty.

The sovereignty is exercised through representative institutions while the people retaining the ultimate power.

2. Form of Government

Proposal:

Sovereignty of the people for governance shall be exercised in the Republic by all delegated authorities in the following manner according to this Constitution. This Constitution is the supreme law of the Republic. Any law or conduct inconsistent with the Constitution or fundamental human rights provisions is invalid. The obligations imposed by it must be fulfilled.

The legislative power of the Republic shall be exercised by the national Parliament, consisting of the National Assembly and the Senate as prescribed in this Constitution. Parliament may seek people's mandate through referendum on important policy matters. The Provincial Councils shall exercise devolved legislative functions as prescribed in this Constitution. Elections for the National Assembly and the Provincial Councils shall be on a mixed system of proportional representation and constituency based first-past-the-post principle within an overall proportional representation.

The judicial power of the Republic shall be exercised by the Supreme Court, the

Constitutional Court, Human Rights Court, the other Courts, Tribunals and Institutions established by this constitution or by law under the Constitution. The independence and impartiality of the judiciary are the cardinal principles. There shall be a Constitutional Court on all matters of the constitution with the powers of post-enactment judicial review.

The executive power of the Republic shall be exercised by the President, the Prime Minister and the Cabinet as prescribed in this Constitution. The devolved executive functions shall be exercised by the Governors, the Chief Ministers and the Council of Minsters as prescribed in this Constitution.

The President of the Republic shall be elected at a national election and be in charge of National Reconciliation and National Security. All other executive powers of the President shall be ceremonial and on the advice of the Prime Minister and the Cabinet. The position of the President is not of an executive president. Head of the Cabinet shall be the Prime Minister. The President shall chair the Cabinet, as Head of the State, only when matters of national reconciliation or national security are discussed or she/he is so invited by the Prime Minister on other matters.

The Provincial Governors of the provinces shall be appointed by the President on the advice of the Prime Minister. The Provincial Councils shall be elected as prescribed in this Constitution and laws under this Constitution. The Governors have special responsibilities on national reconciliation and national security. All other executive powers of the Governors shall be ceremonial and on the Advice of the Chief Ministers and the Council of Ministers. Head of the Council of Ministers shall be the Chief Minister.

Rationale:

The proposed form of government is Parliamentary. Nevertheless, the President shall be nationally elected like in Ireland and shall have responsibilities for 'national security and national reconciliation.' The latter is proposed considering the specific situation in Sri Lanka after the war: (1) continued requirement of 'national security' and (2) the pressing need for 'reconciliation' in its broadest meaning of the term. The placing of both tasks in one position might be the best as they are interrelated. The position of the President is the best, as elected by the whole nation and divorced from the 'political' Cabinet. Cooperation and/or cohabitation between the President and the PM is necessary.

This proposal prefixes the form of government reiterating principle of sovereignty and constitutionalism and eliminates the most obnoxious negation of the supremacy of constitutionalism in Articles 16, 80 (3) and 84. The justification is clear.

The proposal also brings provincial councils into the explanation of legislative power of the republic. This is due recognition of the second tier of governance. As part of the form of government it is important to spell out the basis of election principles.

Independence of the judiciary is established with post-enactment judicial review by the Constitutional Court. Two new additions to the court system are the Constitutional Court and the Human Rights Court. Both are specialties, final review shall be by the Supreme Court as necessary. The executive power is explained after the judiciary, not before. First the basic principles and the institutions, bringing the provincial executive also into the equation. The Governors of the provinces are linked to the President also with responsibilities on 'national security' and 'reconciliation.' Both the President and the Governors are nominal in all other respects.

3. Basic Structure of the Constitution

Proposal:

The basic structure and contents of the constitution could be as follows.

Preamble
Chapter I: The People, the State and Sovereignty
Chapter II: Fundamental Human Rights and Freedoms
Chapter III: Fundamental Duties of the State, Political Parties and Citizens
Chapter IV: Buddhism and Religions
Chapter V: Official Language and Language Rights
Chapter VI: Citizenship and Citizenship Rights
Chapter VII: The National Legislature (Parliament): The National Assembly
Chapter VIII: The National Legislature (Parliament): The Senate
Chapter IX: The National Executive: The President, the Prime Minister and the Cabinet
Chapter X: The Provincial Legislatures: The Provincial Councils
Chapter XI: The Provincial Executives: The Governors, the Chief Ministers and the Council of Ministers
Chapter XII: The Local Government System: Powers and Functions
Chapter XIII: Franchise, Elections and Referendum
Chapter XIV: Basic Principles of the Electoral System: National, Provincial and Local
Chapter XV: Independence of the Judiciary
Chapter XVI: Structure, Functions and Appointment of the Judiciary

Chapter XVIII: The Supreme Courts and the Court of Appeal
Chapter XVII: The Constitutional Court and the Human Rights Court
Chapter XVIII: Public Finance and Fiscal Devolution (including Finance Commission)
Chapter XIX: Constitutional Council and Independent Commissions
Chapter XX: The Public Service: National, Provincial and Local
Chapter XXI: The Public Security
Chapter XXII: International Relations and External Affairs
Chapter XXIII: Interpretation, Amendment and Repeal of the Constitution
    A model for a Preamble is proposed below.

Proposed Preamble

We the People of Sri Lanka,
In order to consolidate national unity, to preserve territorial integrity and peace, to enhance democracy and good governance, to ensure social justice to all communities, to promote social and gender equality, to further promote general welfare and social security of citizens and inhabitants,
Believing in unity in diversity, and
Being a member of the family of democratic nations,
Hereby establish this Constitution,
On the basis of fundamental human rights, people's inalienable sovereignty, constitutionalism and rule of law, compulsory adult universal franchise, and equality of all citizens irrespective of ethnicity, gender, religion, language, political opinion or any other distinction.
This Constitution is supreme and is the fundamental law of the country.

Rationale:

Continuity and discontinuity should be the principles that should be followed in the structure of the constitution. It is highly recommended that there should be an operational Preamble. A draft is given. It proposes a Vision and Basic Principles for a constitution in a plural society with threats and anxieties. The vision is presented taken into consideration the difficulties of constitution making in 'divided societies' (See Foreword) and proposing 'contrasting principles.' The interest and concerns of the majority and minority communities are taken into consideration. On the one hand, 'national unity,' and 'territorial integrity' and on the other hand 'justice to all communities' and 'social equality' are emphasized. The concepts such as 'unity in diversity' and 'membership in the global community' are introduced for the first time.

First chapter is proposed on the same title as in the 1972 and the 1978 constitutions. Then should come the 'Fundamental Human Rights.' Emphasis on 'human' is introduced to 'fundamental rights.' This should continue even as an educational device.

Instead of a chapter on 'Directive Principles of State Policy and Fundamental Duties' 'Fundamental Duties of the State and Citizens' is proposed. Rationale is to emphasize that the State do have 'fundamental duties' and so do the citizens. This is more effective than vague pronouncements under 'directive principles.'

Chapter on Buddhism is retained however renamed as 'Buddhism and Religions' allowing the recognition of other religions. It is placed after the chapter on 'fundamental human rights' and also the 'fundamental duties' for more clarity. Instead of just 'language' the chapter title is proposed as 'official language' also to include 'language rights' in the same chapter. Likewise, the chapter on 'citizenship' should go with the 'citizenship rights.' Chapters on the 'legislature' and the 'executive' go stage by stage for the national and the provincial arrangements. The contents should be clear and elaborate as the titles suggest. A new chapter is proposed to cover the 'local government system' emphasizing the importance, powers and functions within the overall democratic architecture. This is new and is the international trend. 'Franchise, elections and referendum' are combined in one chapter unlike in the present constitution. A new chapter is proposed to lay down the 'basic principles of the electoral system' for the national, provincial and the local elections.'

The provisions for the judiciary is proposed to be more elaborate with emphasis on 'independence of the judiciary.' Four chapters are proposed beginning with the 'independence of the judiciary.' After the 'structure, functions and the procedure to appoint the judiciary,' the setup of the 'Supreme Court and the Court of Appeal' could be explained without diluting the position under the nomenclature 'the superior courts.' What is proposed new are the 'Constitutional Court' and the 'Human Rights Court.' Rationale for these will be explained under the judiciary.

Chapter on 'Finance' needs to be looked into carefully. Expert opinion should be sought. It is proposed to call it 'Public Finance and Fiscal Devolution.' The most important is the role of Parliament in financial control in respect of 'public finance.' Equally important might be to constitutionalize funding formulae for the provincial councils and local governments to ensure fiscal devolution. In this respect, the role of the Finance Commission should be brought into the picture. The 'Constitutional Council and the Independent Commissions' should be one new chapter. The chapter on 'Public Service' needs to be looked into carefully. At present, it is appallingly out of gear. Principles for the public service at the national, provincial and local levels should be laid down. It is also proposed to have a chapter on 'International Relations and External Affairs.' This is a sphere where constitutional provisions needs to be worked out.

4. Citizenship, Religion, Fundamental Rights and Duties, Language Rights, Individual and Group Rights, Directive Principles on State Policy[93]

Proposals:

(a) Citizenship

There shall be one status of citizenship known as the 'citizen of Sri Lanka.' All distinctions as to the way that citizenship was/is acquired by 'descent' or by 'registration' should be eliminated for all purposes, public or private. No discrimination is permitted.

No citizen of Sri Lanka shall be deprived of her/his citizenship except under the law and by order of the Constitutional Court. The Citizenship Act should be so revised.

All citizens who migrate or have already migrated to other countries are encouraged to retain their citizenship or apply for dual citizenship. Their continued contribution to Sri Lanka is appreciated.

Those who have dual citizenship may acquire the right to be a candidate in a local, provincial or national election after six months from making a statutory declaration before the Constitutional Council provided that all other conditions are fulfilled under the elections and other laws. All duel citizens are entitled to all other fundamental rights i.e. freedom of expression, political participation etc. while they reside in the country.

(b) Religion

There can be a chapter on "Buddhism and Religions" as suggested in the "Basic Structure of the Constitution" although it is not ideal. It should however come after the chapter on "Fundamental Human Rights" and also after the proposed "Fundamental Duties of the State and Citizens." A secular constitution/state would have been the best. However, given the

---

[93] There was no alternative for the author, other than lumping all the topic together, as it was the way proposed by the PRC. Otherwise, each topic requires separate attention.

prevailing conditions, there can be other ways of sobering one religion, however important, emerging as a state religion or discriminating others. The following formulation is a suggestion.

The Republic of Sri Lanka recognizes the historical importance of Buddhism and its foremost contribution to the country's social and cultural formation and it shall be the duty of the State to protect Buddhism without any discrimination to other religions.

(c) Fundamental Rights and Duties

It is proposed not to combine 'rights and duties' in one chapter or make one dependent on the other, particularly rights on duties. Only a link can be made. The present proposer is strongly (academically) convinced on the matter although not elaborated here. It is suggested to call "Fundamental Human Rights and Freedoms" and not 'fundamental rights.' 'Freedoms' are suggested to be added as in the 2000 draft. Proposed contents for a chapter on "Fundamental Human Rights" is in Chapter 13.

(d) Language Rights

The new constitution should avoid discriminatory formulations such as "Tamil shall also be an official language" (13th Amendment). There can be a chapter on "Official Language and Language Rights." It is proposed to include English as an official language along with Sinhalese and Tamil. The proposer differs on the prevailing interpretations of 'official' and 'national' languages. English can be an 'official language' but not a 'national language.' An 'official language' has only a legal and an administrative meaning. 'National languages' does have a historical/ cultural meaning. Some of the proposed contents could be as follows.

The official languages of Sri Lanka shall be Sinhalese, Tamil and English. Sinhalese and Tamil shall also be national languages to mean indigenous to the people while recognizing the families/ communities using English as 'mother tongue.'

Any citizen of Sri Lanka shall be entitled to communicate with the public service for any official matter in any of the official languages, Sinhalese, Tamil or English of her/ his choice. The public servants are obliged to communicate with such citizens in the same language provided that some of the official documents could be supplied in the language that they are available at the time with an unofficial translation pertaining to the particular matter, inquiry or request.

All citizens are entitled to use their 'mother tongue'[94] or the language that they are comfortable with in making complaints or statements at police stations, human rights

---

[94] Mother Tongue in Sri Lanka can be either Sinhalese, Tamil or English.

commission or any such institutions and those should be recorded in that language. All citizens are entitled to appear and make submissions before Courts, tribunals or such legal proceedings in their 'mother tongue' or the language they are comfortable with.

A Member of Parliament, a Member of a Provincial Council or a Member of a Local Government shall be entitled to perform her/his duties and discharge functions in Parliament, Provincial Council or Local Government in any of the official languages, Sinhalese, Tamil or English of her/his choice provided that common sense for effective communication should prevail.

A person shall be entitled to be educated through the medium of any of the official or national languages, Sinhalese, Tamil or English. Considering however the pedagogical importance of 'mother tongue' for the formative development of children, the State shall provide and promote education particularly in Sinhalese and Tamil in schools as relevant with gradually promoting English knowledge in every school.

Every child is entitled to sit for public examinations i.e. GCE (O/L or A/L) or any other legally proclaimed examination in any of the official languages, Sinhalese, Tamil or English.

The determination of the medium of instruction in faculties, departments or courses/subjects shall be left for the relevant Institutions of Higher Education provided where one national language is the medium of instruction (Sinhalese or Tamil), the other national language (Sinhalese or Tamil) shall also be made available as a medium of instruction for those who obtain admission to that institution in that language (Sinhalese or Tamil) as the medium of instruction. This does not apply where the medium of instruction is determined as English for pedagogical purposes.

The State shall promote and support the progressive implementation of English as the main medium of instruction in all institutions of higher education to make the graduates of all degree courses equivalent to international standards and suitable for competitive professional opportunities.

(e) Individual and Group Rights

It is difficult to place human rights strictly into one or the other side of the ledger, as individual or group rights. Most of them overlap. Seemingly group rights prove individual, and vice versa. For example, freedom of the press is both an individual right at the level of the journalist, and a group right at the level of a media institution. The right to use one's mother tongue in courts, seemingly a group right of an ethnicity, in operation is an individual right. It is best that the proposed constitution does not make a clear distinction. There should not be separate sections on 'individual rights' and 'group rights.' More relevant is addressing the economic, social and cultural rights going beyond the traditional civil and political rights.

(f) Directive Principles on State Policy

As it was proposed in the "Basic Structure of the Constitution" it would be better to put them more positively as "Fundamental Duties of the State" combining with the "Duties of the Citizens." Some of the proposed formulations could be as follows.

Constitution and Country

It is the primary duty of the State, all state institutions and representatives/officials to recognize the Constitution as the supreme and fundamental law of the country and obey its provisions. All political parties, non-governmental sectors and all citizens are obliged to do the same while retaining the freedom to peacefully criticize and seek changes to its provisions in part or as a whole.

It is the duty of the State to protect and preserve sovereignty, territorial integrity and national unity of the country. All political parties, non-governmental sectors and all citizens are obliged to do the same while retaining the freedom to peacefully differ, criticize and seek changes to the policies of the State in respect of the above.

Social and Ethnic Harmony

It is the duty of the State to promote national unity among the people, build ethnic and religious reconciliation and harmony and maintain peace and stability in the country. All political parties, non-governmental sectors and all citizens are obliged to do the same while retaining the freedom to peacefully differ, criticize and seek changes to the policies of the State in respect of the above.

It is the duty of the State to recognize the diversity of cultures, customs and practices and protect them as far as they are not in breach of the constitution, laws or the cultures, customs and practices of others. It is the duty of the State to promote multiculturalism in the country, set out its policies and at the same time promote Sri Lankan identity above and over multiculturalism. All political parties, non-government sectors and all citizens are obliged to do the same while retaining the freedom to peacefully differ, criticize and seek changes to the policies and practices of the State in respect of the above.

The State shall not promote in any manner ethno-nationalism in the country directly or indirectly. On the contrary, the State shall promote civic nationalism and liberal patriotism based on most enlightened religious and secular principles, fundamental human rights, and cosmopolitanism. The State shall launch educational programs, formal and informal, to promote the above. All political parties, non-government sectors and all citizens are obliged to do the same and participate in such educational programs at will while retaining the freedom to peacefully differ, criticize and seek changes to the policies and practices of the State in respect of the above.

Social Justice, Equity and Poverty Alleviation

It is the duty of the State to ensure and promote social justice in all spheres of economic, social, political, civil and cultural life of the people taking inspirations and guidelines from international human rights and democratic norms and strictly following the 'fundamental human rights and freedoms' chapter in the Constitution. It is the duty of all political parties, non-governmental sectors and all citizens to do the same while retaining the freedom to peacefully differ, criticize and seek changes to the policies and practices of the State in respect of the above.

The State has special obligations to alleviate poverty and look after the poor and the marginalized in society. It is the duty of the State to promote policies and programs to bridge the gaps between the rich and the poor and promote equitable income distribution throughout the society and the country as much as possible. The State should seek the cooperation of the private sector and all sections of the society to develop the economy and society, in a sustainable and equitable manner and it is the duty of the private sector, all political parties, other sectors of society and all citizens to support the State in these ventures while retaining the freedom to peacefully differ, criticize and seek changes to such policies and practices.

Children, Women, Elderly and Disabled

The State has special obligations to look after the rights and welfare of the children, women, elderly and people with disability. It is the duty of all political parties, non-governmental sectors, private enterprises and all citizens to support such efforts and likewise look after the rights and welfare of the children, women, elderly and people with disability within families and in society.

Free Education and Health Care

It is the duty of the State to maintain and promote free education including higher education with the cooperation of the private sector as necessary. It is also the duty of the State to maintain and promote free healthcare and hospitals with the cooperation of the private sector as necessary. The public private partnership (PPP) should be the norm. On both education and health, the State should determine target allocations from the annual budgets from time to time. When citizens offer education or health in the private sector, the State should ensure that those services are affordable. The State should have a national medical drugs policy to ensure all necessary medical drugs are affordable and available. It is the duty of all political parties, non-governmental sectors, the private sector and all citizens to support the policies and programs of the State on free education and health care as much as possible while retaining the freedom to peacefully differ, criticize and seek changes to such policies and programs.

Welfare and Social Services

It is the duty of the State to maintain and promote general welfare and assistance services as necessary to the citizens without any political or any other partiality through the national services, provincial councils or local government institutions. These should be announced in national, provincial and local government budgets and policies. It is the duty of all political parties, non-government sectors and all citizens to support such efforts while retaining the freedom to peacefully differ, criticize and seek changes to such policies and programs. It is the prerogative of all citizens not only to obtain these services as necessary but also to support them through voluntary work or any other means.

Environmental Protection

It is the primary responsibility of the State to protect the environment within its territory, land and offshore, in line with international standards and efforts, and reduce greenhouse gas emissions. It is the duty of all political parties, non-governmental sectors including the private enterprises and all citizens to do the same and support the efforts of the State in those ventures while retaining the freedom to peacefully differ, criticize and seek changes to the policies and practices of the State.

Personal Security, Law and Order

It is the primary duty of the State to maintain law and order and ensure social and personal security of citizens through effective and citizen's friendly police service/s and other law enforcement agencies particularly preventing robbery, theft, crime and violence in society. It is the duty of all political parties, non-governmental sectors and all citizens to cooperate with the State, the police service/s and other law enforcement agencies in preventing robbery, theft, crime and violence in society while retaining the freedom to peacefully differ, criticize and seek changes to the policies and practices of the State, the police service/s and other law enforcement agencies in this respect.

Duties of Public Servants

It is the primary duty of all State officials including the police officers to serve the citizens, be polite to them, and maintain the best professional standards and refrain from favoritism, nepotism or any kind of monetary or other misdeeds. It is the duty of all political parties, non-governmental sectors and all citizens to extend cooperation to state officials, follow all relevant rules in dealing with them and refrain from trying to influence them politically or in any other respect while retaining the freedom to peacefully raise issues, stand for one's rights or peacefully differ, criticize and seek changes to the public services and practices as relevant.

Duties of Political Parties and Leaders

It is the duty of all political parties to be democratic in their policies and organizational structures, maintain high professional standards and refrain from nepotism, and any kind of monetary or other misdeeds. It is the duty of political party leaders to be accountable to their members, party organizations and maintain transparent and accountable practices for campaign funding and refrain from nepotism or any unethical practices.

It is the duty of all political parties, politicians, national, provincial or local, to maintain high standards of professional ethics and refrain from favoritism, nepotism and any kind of monetary or other misdeeds. It is the duty of the State to have codes of ethics for all members of parliament, provincial councilors, and local government representatives.

Duties of Citizens

It is the duty of all citizens to be respectful to each other, recognize each other's dignity and rights, be reasonable and rational in all dealings with the state officials or fellow citizens and refrain from violent or aggressive behavior at all times. All politicians, citizens and media personnel should refrain from hate speech or expressions that could lead to incitement or social disharmony.

Please note that the duties to respect human rights including 'economic and social rights' and freedoms are not included here as they can be more effectively protected and implemented through a 'Fundamental Human Rights and Freedoms' chapter. All legally enshrined fundamental human rights automatically generate necessary duties.

5. Legislature (Unicameral or Bicameral)

Proposal:

The national legislature shall be bicameral both for the reasons of devolution and otherwise. The national Parliament should consist of two chambers: National Assembly or the lower house and the Senate, the upper house. It should consist of 36 members, one half of them or 18 members nominated 2 each by provincial councils (one female and one male) and the other half or 18 members nominated by the President on the advice of the Prime Minister to represent unrepresented sections of society (i.e. special minorities) and professional groups/interests and 9 members strictly being women. The term of office of the Senate should be 3 years only, one half retiring after 18 months at the beginning. All members should be over 40 years of age, with professional and/or personal integrity not involved in active politics and qualify to be elected only twice.

The terms and functions of the Senate could be similar to the Senate under the 1947 constitution as revised to suit the present conditions. However, no minister should be appointed from the Senate and tasks of the Senate purely should be legislative and policy. Policy inputs on human rights, reconciliation, devolution, public finance and social justice, and also the people's grievances should be the main tasks.

Rationale:

The Senate is proposed to have a sobering effect on the lower house. It should be a part of checks and balances in the legislature. The members should have expertise or interest in legislative and/or financial matters. The Senate should particularly safeguard the interests of the provinces. The Senate however should not be a chamber of filibustering. After referring a bill to the Senate it should dispose of it within 3 months or 1 month in the case of a national budget or financial bill so determined by the Speaker.

6. Supremacy of Constitution or Parliament?

Proposal:

Parliament should not be declared as supreme by any means. The Constitution should be declared as supreme following the basic tenets of constitutionalism. The legislature, the executive and even the judiciary should work and operate under the constitution. The 'duties on the part of the State, political parties and citizens' on 'constitutionalism' were proposed previously. Supremacy of the constitution should be pronounced at the very beginning of the Constitution. The interpretation of the Constitution should be left only to the judiciary (Constitutional Court and any appeal going to the Supreme Court in special circumstances) so design to ensure its impartiality, professionalism and integrity in all its matters.

Rationale:

The accorded supremacy of parliament has been the curse of the country. It has led to the assumption of supremacy by unscrupulous politicians.

7. Separation of Powers

Proposal:

'Separation of powers' should not be declared in the constitution. It could be implicit as necessary than explicit.

Rationale:

Even in the United States it was not declared as such even after a proposal by James Madison.

8. Independence of the Judiciary

Proposal:

Independence of the Judiciary should be 'absolute.' To ensure that independence, while provisions should be made for the independent, impartial and qualified appointments, the professional caliber of the legal profession should be uplifted at the source level of legal education and training.

To ensure impartial and professional appointments based on merit, the caliber of the President and her/his standing above partisan politics is important.

Rationale:

Independence of the judiciary is of paramount importance for safeguarding human rights of citizens, democracy as the governing system and to ensure a just society.

The record of the judiciary has been appalling since 1970s due to political or bad appointments or some of the persons themselves babbling in politics.

9. Constitutional Court

Proposal:

Constitutional Court can be of 7 members, 6 appointed by an 'impartial and above politics President,' selected out of the judges (retired or sitting) of the Supreme Court or the High Courts on submission of applications or 'written expression of interest.' The Chief Justice shall be the ex-officio Chair of the Constitutional Court.

The main function of the Constitutional Court is to decide and determine on all constitutional issues referred to it by the President, the Prime Minister, the Speakers of the National Assembly or the Senate or any of the Governors or the Chief Ministers of Provincial Councils. Such a request also can be made by any other court to the Constitutional Court. There will be a legal committee attached to the Constitutional Court to screen those referred issues to determine their legal veracity.

No proceedings or functions of the Parliament or the Provincial Councils should be halted by the mere fact that a matter has been referred to unless the Constitutional Council so determines.

Rationale:

There can be issues of controversy with a New Constitution or even otherwise especially related to the devolution of power. The Constitutional Court also can be a safeguard to prevent the center taking over the powers of the provincial councils.

10. Power Sharing, Devolution and Local Government

Proposal:

'Shared Responsibility' and 'Cooperative Devolution' should be the concepts. The 'shared responsibility' is a growing concept with the UN endorsement. Rather than 'power,' what should be emphasized is justice and sharing of responsibility for governance. 'Power sharing' is an old and elitist concept, developed for the convenience of the 'elite' and the politicians who thrive on conflict. The inclusion of the concept of 'power' into the equation would create endless controversy and strive for power on all sides. By giving power or 'sense of power' to the provincial councils, a new layer of parasitic politicians have emerged particularly in the South.

'Shared responsibility' by different political parties representing different ethnic or religious communities should be built politically. 'Unity governments,' 'coalitions' or 'united fronts' could be the political mechanisms. However, the constitution cannot or should not spell them out. A scheme of devolution is not proposed here. A proposal will be sent later.[95] In essence, devolution should come closer to federalism. Local government should be enshrined in the Constitution and it should be a Chapter not with details but with vision, principles and main contours. (See Chapter 14).

Rationale:

---

[95] It should be noted that no separate proposal was sent on this matter to the PRC while various guidelines were elaborated in various articles published by the author.

Sri Lanka should not go back on devolution, but forward. Devolution should come closer to federalism preventing the central government 'giving from one hand and taking from the other.' Even at present these aberrations are in operation. Local government is an important institution in democracy. New initiatives for constitution making incorporate local government in constitutions. LG's are the closest to the people and the full potential is not utilized at present.

11. 'Sharing Power' at the Centre

Proposal:

Although 'sharing power' is mentioned here, as it mainly means how to enlist and encourage the participation of 'minority' political parties and communities (Tamil, Muslim and Christian) in governance, it is proposed to mention some guidelines for the inclusion of those parties or representatives in a Cabinet. Inclusive governance also means the participation of women. In addition to the preservation of an overall PR system for parliamentary elections and the new introduction of a Senate, the following is proposed as an example.

The Prime Minister shall recommend to the President the names and assignments of Cabinet and other Ministers to be appointed, the number not exceeding 30 to the Cabinet, and not exceeding 60 in total, giving due consideration to create a representative and/or consensual government of different communities also representing an adequate number of women.

Rationale:

It is obvious that an inclusive system of government or a consensual system of governance cannot be created by a constitution per se. It is left for higher level of democratic politics. The above however can be a guideline which could be put into practice through negotiation and compromise.

12. 'Constitutional Council' and Independent Commissions

Proposal:

The name 'Constitutional Council' appears to be a misnomer. It should not be confused with the Constitutional Court in the public eye. The better name might be "Higher Appointments Council." The Higher

Appointments Council can be of 9 members. Only 3 being ex-officio: The Speaker, the Prime Minister and the Leader of the Opposition. The other 6 members shall be appointed by the President from an equal number of 6 names each proposed by the Speaker, the Prime Minister and the Leader of the Opposition. The names proposed shall be of high calibre, with professional integrity and experience, the age not less than 40 and not less than 2 of them to represent minority communities. At least 2 of the nominees shall be women.

The Higher Appointments Council shall appoint all Independent Commissions on the basis of written expression of interest. It shall also appoint all Heads of Departments and Institutions such as the Attorney General, Auditor General and the IGP etc. on specific criteria developed by the Council with or without the expression of interest. It can be 60 percent merit and 40 percent seniority. The appointment of Heads of the Army, Navy and the Air Force is left to the President.

Rationale: Hopefully self-evident from the proposal.

13. Public Service

Proposal:

The public service should completely be independent from politics, partisan or otherwise, at the national, provincial or local government level. This does not mean that certain categories of public servants should not have political rights. However, they should keep the two separately. All public servants should have the right to join a trade union or a professional association as the case may be.

The present provisions of Chapter IX should be completely overhauled. The present provision says that "Subject to the provisions of the Constitution, the appointment, transfer, dismissal and disciplinary control of public officers is hereby vested in the Cabinet of Ministers, and all public officers shall hold office at pleasure." The nature of the present provisions itself requires a New Constitution!

The appointment, transfer, dismissal and disciplinary control of public officers shall be under the Independent Public Services Commission (PSC). Some powers and functions could be delegated to the Heads of Departments under the supervision of the PSC. The Minister can appoint Permanent Secretaries to their Ministries. They should not influence the other appointments in the public service directly or indirectly. There should be reform and regeneration of the public service. This should be primarily achieved through education and training which are beyond the purview of the constitution making. However, certain principles could be laid down.

Rationale:

Political interference in the public service is a vexed problem. The recent most issue that the Minister of Higher Education is embroiled in, is only a tip of the iceberg. It is also the primary cause for the degeneration of the political culture in Sri Lanka where people go behind politicians not to ameliorate grievances but seeking favors. This is also the root cause of nepotism and fraud that also leads to thuggery and violence in maintaining the status quo of political interferences or predominance. Public Service should be completely overhauled including the Foreign Service.

14. Electoral Reforms

Proposal:

An overall PR system should be retained while reintroducing the single member or multi-member seats under the FPP for the election of Parliament. However, the 'best-loser formula' should not be adopted for the national, the provincial or the local government elections. This is simply not democratic. This has unfortunately crept into the President's Manifesto in January 2015 and this is also the formula in the Local Government Elections Reform Act of 2012 with other regressive elements.

It is possible to introduce a FPP seats system within an overall PR system as I have elaborated elsewhere without increasing the number of Members of Parliament beyond 225. In view of the introduction of a Senate or even otherwise, increasing the number is not necessary. What is necessary is the 'increase' of the quality of members and their commitment. The Code of Ethics is a must. For the local government system, a simple ward system might be the most appropriate with the objective of reducing partisan politics and enhancing consensual policy making as much as possible.

Rationale:

The rationale for the above proposal is given in Chapters 10 and various other articles.

15. Judicial Review of Legislation

Proposal:

It is important that the consistency of legislation is reviewed by the judiciary. This is one basic principle of constitutionalism. Post enactment judicial review should be reintroduced. Any citizen or organization/entity should be able to challenge legislation or some provisions of legislation before the proposed Constitutional Court. This is a fundamental right of citizens. Until a verdict is given, the legislation should prevail unless an injunction is sought in the case of personal grievance or damage.

Rationale:

The abolition of constitutional review has led to many aberrations in the legal and the justice system. Even before, there have been aberrations (1956 Official Languages Act) due to partiality or political influence. Most vulnerable have been the minorities. Especially in view of devolution of power, the judicial review of legislation should be re-introduced.

16. Powers of President under Parliamentary System

Proposal:

The President shall be in charge of national reconciliation and national security. All other executive powers of the President shall be ceremonial and on the advice of the Prime Minister and the Cabinet. The position of the President is not of an executive president. Head of the Cabinet shall be the Prime Minister. The President shall chair the Cabinet, as Head of the State, only when matters of national reconciliation or national security are discussed or she/he is so invited by the Prime Minister on other matters. The President should be above politics after election and should resign from any party affiliation after election.

Rationale:

Sri Lanka should not move from one extreme to the other. The position of the President even after the abolition of the executive presidency should be made for good use. There is much reason to leave Security and Reconciliation in the charge of a President, given that the war is over but reconciliation and security still remains major concerns. There is much to be done, and the President and his/her office/staff will be in a better position than any minister to deal with the tasks of reconciliation.

17. Election of President under the Parliamentary System

Proposal:

President should be elected nationally as it is.

Rationale:

There is merit in an elected President as a symbol of national unity. The minorities have a better say in electing a President as shown in January 2015 and other elections. It would be easy for minorities or the Northern/Eastern Provincial Councils to deal with a non-executive President than a political Prime Minister or a Cabinet. Ireland is a successful example of having an elected President in a parliamentary democracy.

18. Public Security

Proposal:

Public security should be under the President. The President shall consult the Prime Minister on all important matters. The President shall appoint the Heads of the Army, the Navy and the Air Force, and the Security Council. He/she shall preside the Security Council, the Prime Minister and another Minister of his choice as members of the Security Council other than all armed forces heads and any other members. All Heads of armed forces and intelligence should report to the President. All Governors of provinces directly accountable to the President and report and assist the President in matters of security and reconciliation. It is the final decision of the President to place or move cantonments or camps or any other establishment of the armed forces from any part of the country depending on security or other considerations.

Rationale:

Proposal can be considered largely self-evident. Security and security of the territorial integrity could be still considered national priorities. It is logical to place both security and reconciliation under the President given interdependence of the two matters.

19. Public Finance (and Fiscal Devolution)

Proposal:

It should be named "Public Finance and Fiscal Devolution" and not merely Finance. Parliament should have full control over public finance at the national level directly or through appointed standing committees. There can be joint committee sessions with the Senate on financial matters as necessary.

There should be fiscal devolution. Not only the provincial councils, but also the local governments should have 'block grants' and 'other grants' directly or through the provincial councils in the latter's case. The ability of the provincial councils and the local governments to device their taxes, rates and levies should be flexible with strict auditing, accounting and accountability procedures. The above are very basic proposals and the PRC or other committees in constitution making could organize seminars/workshops or specialist consultations to seek further views.

Rationale:

'Public finance management' can be considered one of the weakest in Sri Lanka. There are many untapped financial resources that could be utilized for social welfare and services for the poor and the needy. The national government should allow creativity and initiatives on the part of the provincial councils and local governments to pursue these avenues.

20. Other Matters

It is proposed not to rush a New Constitution.

The PRC should focus not only on 'soft' or much discussed areas such as 'presidential system vs. parliamentary system' but 'hard' areas such as 'public finance,' 'fiscal devolution,' 'public service' etc. It is proposed to conduct more focused consultations with specialist on these matters.

For example, in seeking views on a chapter on 'International Relations and External Affairs' the views of the present or former diplomats could be sought. In revising the chapters on 'Public Finance' or "Public Service,' views of the present and former senior public servants should be sought. It is strongly proposed that a 'Code of Ethics' should be included in the New Constitution as a Schedule.

12
Proposed Chapter on
Fundamental Human Rights and Freedoms

1. Right to Life

All citizens of Sri Lanka have the inherent right to life. This right shall be protected by law under all circumstances.

Sri Lanka shall not impose capital punishment for any crime, but impose appropriate and well-defined punishments as deterrence and prevention.

2. Nature of Rights

All citizens have liberty and security of person, and entitled to privacy. They are free and equal, individually or collectively, in dignity and fundamental human rights enshrined or implied in this constitution irrespective of race, ethnicity, religion, gender, language, caste, economic status, sexual preference, political opinion or any other distinction.

They are endowed with reason and conscience and shall act towards one another in a spirit of brotherhood and responsibility.

3. Freedom of Thought, Conscience and Religion

Every person in Sri Lanka is entitled to freedom of thought, conscience and religion, including the freedom to have, practice or to adopt a religion or belief of her/his free choice.

No one shall be prohibited or discriminated for wearing attire prescribed by one's own religion or belief.

4. Freedom from Torture

No person in Sri Lanka shall be subject to torture or to cruel, inhuman or degrading treatment or punishment. The police and the armed forces have special responsibilities in safeguarding this freedom from torture of the citizens.

5. Right to Equality

All citizens are equal before the law and are entitled to the equal protection of the law.

No one shall be discriminated against on the grounds of race, ethnicity, religion, language, caste, gender, sexual orientation, political opinion, place of birth or any such grounds.

No person on the above grounds shall be subject to any restriction or condition with regard to access to public and open amenities (shops, restaurants, hotels, play grounds etc.) unless they are by law declared as private places, or religious places limited to their own members or adherents.

Nothing in this Article shall prevent affirmative action or provision made under law for the advancement of children, women, disabled and the needy or marginalized sections of society. Reasonable language, educational or other requirements necessary for employment, professions or services shall not be interpreted to mean discrimination.

6. Freedom from Arbitrary Arrest, Detention and Punishment

No person shall be arrested except according to the due process of law. In case of arrest, she/he shall be informed of the reasons of arrest at the time of arrest.

Every person held in custody, detained or otherwise deprived of personal liberty shall be brought before the judge of the nearest competent court according to procedure established by law, and shall not be further held in custody, detained or deprived of personal liberty except upon and in terms of the order of such judge made in accordance with procedure established by law.

Any person charged with an offence shall be entitled to be heard, in person or by an attorney-at-law, at a fair trial by a competent court.

No person shall be punished by death.

No person shall be punished by imprisonment except by order of a competent court, made in accordance with procedure established by law. The arrest, holding in custody, detention or other deprivation of personal liberty of a person, pending investigation or trial, shall not be executed as punishment.

Every person shall be presumed innocent until she/he is proved guilty. However it is the duty of such persons to cooperate with investigations.

No person shall be held guilty of an offence on account of any act or omission which did not, at the time of such act or omission, constitute an offence or crime, according to the national laws or to the general principles of law recognized by the community of nations. No penalty shall be imposed for any offence more severe than the penalty in force at the time such offence was committed.

7. Freedom of Speech, Expression, Media and Academic Freedom

All citizen shall have the right to hold opinions without interference.

Every citizen shall have the right to freedom of expression including publication. This right shall include freedom to seek, receive and impart information, ideas and knowledge of all kinds, either orally, in writing, in print or electronically, in the form of art or through any other media with social and personal responsibility.

All academics broadly defined as part of the larger community shall have academic freedom for the promotion of teaching, research and knowledge with social and personal responsibility.

All journalists broadly defined as part of the larger community shall have media freedom for the promotion of information, news, justice and social awareness with social and personal responsibility.

Freedom of expression shall not be abused by anyone to propagate war, advocacy of ethnic or religious hatred that constitutes incitement to hostility, conflict or violence. Other restrictions on freedom of speech and expression shall be explicit and shall only be as provided by law for the respect of the rights and reputation of others, or for the protection of national security, ethnic and religious harmony, public order or public protection in the country.

8. Freedom of Association and Assembly

Every citizen has the right to freedom of association with others and peaceful assembly.

The freedom of association includes the right to form and join trade unions for the protection of employment, wages and working conditions. There can be lawful restrictions for certain categories of employees to form or join trade unions i.e. armed forces.

Every citizen has the right to engage by herself/himself or in association with others in any lawful occupation, profession, trade, business or enterprise.

The freedom of association also includes the right to form employers' federations or such organizations for the protection of private enterprises or companies.

Every citizen has the right to form or join associations to promote political objectives or cultural, language or religious interests.

There can be laws promoting the registration of all such associations while the registration is primarily voluntary except in the case of political parties for electoral purposes.

All associations shall govern by the prevailing laws and when there are conflicts, particularly in the case of trade unions, those shall be resolved through collective bargaining or through judicial procedures.

In peaceful assembly, every citizen shall refrain from violence and damage to property or any undue obstruction to day to day life of other citizens.

9. Freedom of Movement

Every citizen has the right to freedom of movement and of choosing her/his residence in any part of Sri Lanka, personally or with family, without disturbing the peaceful living of others.

The freedom of movement includes the right to seek employment abroad or to lawfully migrate to another country temporarily or permanently subject to relevant international laws or laws of those countries. Such citizens have the freedom to return to Sri Lanka and/or seek dual citizenship.

10. Right to Work

Every citizen has the right and responsibility to work. This means the opportunity to gain her/his living by work that she/he freely chooses or accepts and to take appropriate steps to gain and safeguard this right.

The realization of this right will depend on the educational, technical and vocational training and guidance that the State can supply in association with the private and the non-governmental sectors and the sustainable economic and social development of the country.

The right to work also includes the right of every working person to have equal remuneration for equal work, in particular between men and women, and safe and favorable conditions of work with reasonable minimum wages and working hours.

11. Right to Education

Every citizen has the right to education and responsibility to seek proper education for oneself. Parents have responsibility to guide children in this respect. Education shall be directed to the realization of gainful employment and to the full development of the human personality and the sense of its dignity and shall strengthen the respect for human rights and responsibilities.

Education, formal and informal, shall enable all citizens to promote understanding, tolerance and friendship among all ethnic and religious communities and shall promote peace and reconciliation, nationally and internationally.

Parents have the right to choose a school for their children and equal opportunities shall prevail.

Education shall be compulsory up to GCE O/L examination, provided in one of the national languages, Sinhalese or Tamil, of parents' choice. Education shall be available free at public schools throughout and all public universities. Anyone may pursue education at private school or private university. Common standards shall prevail. The State shall provide technical and vocational education as appropriate to those who cannot enter university or seek employment otherwise.

The State shall expand free university education. University education shall be suitable to employment opportunities including competence in English.

12. Right to Health Care

Every citizen has the right to the enjoyment of the highest attainable standard of physical and mental health. Towards the realization of this right the State shall provide the following provisions:

For the healthy development of the child including the reduction of the stillbirth-rate and of infant mortality;

For the medical care of the mother particularly during pregnancy and after;

The improvement of all aspects of environmental and industrial hygiene;

The prevention, treatment and control of epidemic, endemic, occupational and other diseases;

The creation of conditions which would assure to all citizens necessary medical service and medical attention in the event of sickness.

Every citizen shall have access to free healthcare, including dental care, and medical services as necessary through public hospitals, clinics and such institutions including free medication to the needy and the poor sectors of society. The State shall continue and expand the public hospitals and health care facilities and provide free health services.

Every citizen has a right to obtain medical drugs at affordable prices. The State shall have a national medical drugs policy to ensure all necessary medical drugs are affordable and available.

13. Cultural Rights

Every citizen has the right, personally or in association with others, to take part in cultural life of Sri Lanka and her/his own community or region. The realization of this right shall include those necessary steps for the uncovering and conservation of the cultural heritage of the country at national, provincial and local levels. Any willful damage or desecration of cultural artefacts or places shall be an infringement of this right.

Every citizen has the right, personally or in association with others, to promote one's own language, literature, culture, traditions and customs however in conformity with human rights of all.

For the cultural promotion of the country and communities, all citizens shall respect the freedom indispensable for creative activities of individuals and groups. Cultural promotion in the country shall attract international respect and promote cultural tourism.

14. Operational Provisions

In interpreting any of the rights or articles of this chapter, the courts may refer to the UN Declaration of Human Rights (UDHR), the International Covenant on Civil and Political Rights (ICCPR) or the International Covenant on Economic, Social and Cultural Rights (ICESCR) or any other international convention.

There shall be a distinction between the application of civil and political rights, on the one hand, and the application of economic and social rights, on the other, enunciated in this chapter.

There shall be a Human Right Court to adjudicate matters pertaining to this chapter on 'Fundamental Human Rights and Freedoms' in addition to the chapter on 'Fundamental Duties of the State, Political Parties and Citizens.'

Every citizen shall be entitled to apply to the Human Rights Court, in respect of any infringement or imminent infringement, by legislative, executive or administrative action, of a fundamental human right enunciated in sections from 1 to 9 to seek personal redress. If the infringement is outside the premises of the public authorities, the Human Rights Court may refer the matter to the Human Rights Commission for redress or settlement.

In respect of economic, social and cultural rights enunciated in sections from 10 to 13, public interest litigation would apply. Nevertheless, only registered trade unions or other associations could file such applications. The purpose of public interest litigation would be to seek policy and/ or administrative improvements or corrections in respect of the absence, non-protection or infringement of those rights. The recommendations of the Human Rights Court in the form of determinations shall be binding on the public institutions, authorities or personnel who are responsible for the promotion and protection of such rights.

13

Proposed Chapter on Local Government System Objects, Structures and Functions[96]

Strong local government is critical for development, democracy, reconciliation and nation building. Sri Lanka shall build on long traditions of local self-government, both ancient and modern. (1) Active engagement and support of individual citizens and communities, (2) partnership of various stakeholders, private and public, and (3) efficient and effective management of local government tasks, underpin successful social and economic development.

The required partnership entails cooperation of central government, provincial councils, private sector, civil society organizations and others, to make the local government objects, structures and functions successful. The developmental local government is the required norm.[97]

---

[96] This chapter is drafted as example, not strictly as formulations. Constitutional recognition of local government is part of 'positive constitutionalism' today. Russia has a brief chapter, and South Africa an extensive one. The reason for an extensive chapter in South Africa is lack of primary legislation. In the presence of several primary legislation, Sri Lanka can have a moderate size chapter to inculcate a new vision and orientation.

[97] On conceptualization of 'developmental local government' see J. W. De Visser, "Developmental Local Government: A Case Study of South Africa" (2005) among others.

Objects

The main objects of local government are:
To provide democratic and accountable government for local communities;

To promote social and economic development;

To foster peace, amity and understanding between communities;

To ensure safe and healthy environment;

To encourage the involvement of communities, community organizations, women and youth in the matters of local governance; and

Any other as prescribed in relevant legislation for Pradeshiya Sabhas, Urban Councils or Municipal Councils.

Structures

Local government is broadly a devolved subject under the Constitution, coming generally under the purview of the provincial councils, provided that no alteration can be made for the structures, powers or functions of the local government system or the electoral system under which those bodies are established.

The provincial councils are entrusted with a key leadership role in guiding the local governments, coordinate them with consent, and promote them for strategic planning and delivering services to the communities efficiently. National funding for local governments shall be channeled through the provincial councils under their supervision while the overall auditing placed under the provincial Auditor General.

There are three main tiers of local government - Pradeshiya Sabhas, Urban Councils and Municipal Councils – the status and demarcations will be reviewed and changed from time to time. Any Pradeshiya Sabha or Urban Council can request an upgrading which will be reviewed and determined under the prevailing laws.

Local government reforms are in order: structural, electoral and managerial.

There shall be an Independent Commission on Local Government to look into structural matters, delimitation of wards, recommend upgrading of council status and make recommendations on the sufficiency or insufficiency of funding sources for local government or any other matter prescribed in relevant legislation. The Commission will report to the Prime Minister and coordinate with the subject Minister and the Provincial Councils.

All local government bodies shall be elected on common electoral principles and a system as prescribed in the Local Authorities Elections Ordinance and as revised or substituted. After the election of competent candidates to represent the wards (single-member or multi-member) under the FPP principle, there shall be twenty five percent of women representation elected on an overall proportional representation (PR) basis.

The main object of the electoral system for local government is to elect competent and reliable candidates to represent the electorate/s based on 'candidate cum party preferences.' Twenty five percent of women representation is ensured as affirmative action considering their social disadvantage in the present social and political environment.

Functions

Pradeshiya Sabhas

Functions of the Pradeshiya Sabhas shall be according to the Pradeshiya Sabhas Act (No. 15 of 1987) as revised or substituted. The functions include inter alia:

(1) To be charged with public utility services, public thoroughfares, building approvals, homestead and town planning in the area;

(2) To engage in socio-economic and agricultural development activities in cooperation with the relevant .provincial council and the national government;

(3) To protect and promote environment within its area under national guidelines including efficient garbage disposal and sewage;

(4) To be charged with the regulation, control and administration of all matters relating to public health in the area in cooperation with the provincial council; and

(5) To be charged generally with the protection and promotion of the comfort, convenience, arts, crafts, sports, entertainment and welfare of the people and all amenities within such area.

Pradeshiya Sabhas also have the authority to engage themselves in public business enterprises along with the private sector and with non-governmental organizations as appropriate. Promotion of tourism can be one of the areas of enterprises.

Urban Councils

Functions of the Urban Councils shall be according to the Urban Councils Ordinance (January 1940) as revised or substituted. The functions include inter alia:

(1) To be charged with public utility services, public thoroughfares, building approvals and urban planning in the area;

(2) To engage in socio-economic development activities in cooperation with the relevant provincial council and the national government;

(3) To facilitate business, industrial and commercial development in the area through efficient services;

(4) To protect and promote environment within its area under national guidelines including efficient garbage disposal and sewage planning;

(5) To be charged with the regulation, control and administration of all matters relating to public health in the area in cooperation with the provincial council;

(6) To be charged generally with the protection and promotion of the comfort, convenience, arts, crafts, sports, entertainment and welfare of the people and all amenities within such area; and

(7) To assist the relevant provincial council and/or the national government in converting the suitable areas into Smart Cities.

Urban Councils also have the authority to engage themselves in public business enterprises along with the private sector and with non-governmental organizations as appropriate. Promotion of tourism can be one of the areas of enterprises.

Municipal Councils

(1) To be charged with public utility services, public thoroughfares, building approvals and city planning in the area; (2) To engage in socio-economic development activities in the municipal areas independently or in cooperation with the relevant provincial council and the national government; (3) To facilitate business, industrial and commercial development in the municipal area through efficient services; (4) To protect and promote environment within its area under national guidelines including efficient garbage disposal and sewage planning; (5) To be charged with the regulation, control and administration of all matters relating to public health in the area in cooperation with the provincial council; (6) To be charged generally with the protection and promotion of the comfort, convenience, arts, crafts, sports, entertainment and welfare of the people

and all amenities within such area; and (7) To assist the relevant provincial council and the national government in converting the suitable areas into Smart Cities or Mega Polis.

Municipal Councils also have the authority to engage themselves in public business enterprises along with the private sector and with non-governmental organizations as appropriate. Promotion of tourism can be one of the areas of enterprises.

Powers

All local government bodies – Pradeshiya Sabhas, Urban Councils and Municipal Councils – shall have executive powers to administer the functions under their respective jurisdictions. Their council meetings shall be geared to making decisions in respect of these functions.

All local government bodies shall have limited legislative powers to make By-Laws under relevant national laws or provincial statutes. There shall be appropriate efficient mechanism to verify and approve or disapprove the consistency with the principal enactments.

All local government bodies also have powers:

(1) To approve budgets; (2) Impose local rates and other taxes, levies and duties in consistent with national legislation and/or with the approval of the Treasury; and   (3) To raise loans as necessary.

There shall be no judicial powers to the local government bodies whatsoever. Powers of all local government bodies (Pradeshiya Sabhas, Urban Councils and Municipal Councils) shall be under the Constitution and according to other national laws.

General Provisions

All local government bodies are entitled to have appropriate funding, as grants, allocated in the national budget, and channeled and monitored through the provincial councils. Such grants shall be based on professionally devised funding or grant formulas.

All local government bodies are entitled to have required and competent officials (administrative, financial and legal) through the consolidated public services. Professional advisory services and experts also should be available for local government bodies in improving their capacities and efficiency as necessary. International cooperation may be sought in the latter category. All local government bodies should adopt a common business excellence framework (i.e. based on 'Malcolm Baldrige' or ABEF).[98]

All local government bodies and relevant officials (elected or employed) are responsible and accountable, personally and collectively, on all financial matters with strict monetary discipline.

In undertaking the respective functions of local government bodies, 'committee system of governance' as prescribed in relevant legislation and above shall be followed.

All local government bodies shall have Citizen Charters and other appropriate measures to promote citizen and community participation in local government activities. The formation of Ward Committees under the auspicious of respective ward members and with the participation of civil society organizations are encouraged. All candidates stood for elections may also participate in such committees.

In the promotion of people's participation, good governance and accountability, and also in encouraging rural awakening, structures similar to 'Grama Rajya' or such models may be formed in Pradeshiya Sabha areas after careful study by the Independent Commission on Local Government.

---

[98] 'Malcolm Baldrige' model was devised in America and is used in several other countries. ABEF is what is prominent in Australia and applied in local government bodies.

PART III

CONSTITUTION MAKING IN PERSPECTIVE

14

Understanding Political Change in 2015

"Never doubt that a small group of thoughtful, committed, citizens can change the world." - Margaret Mead

In recent debates on Sri Lanka's future and required political change, academics and political analysts have extensively discussed constitutional and governance issues,[99] but not so much matters related to 'political culture' or 'electoral behavior.' There has been some understanding for some time that the key ideology that influences the political behavior of political leaders as well as the general public has been 'nationalism,' of various varieties and different types,[100] but no particular studies have been conducted to ascertain their influence on electoral behavior in recent times.[101] Much of the prognosis on the adversarial effects of nationalism/s in the country was related to 'linguistic nationalism',[102] 'ethno-

---

*Many thanks to Prema-chandra Athukorala (Australian National University) for his clarifications on P. Athukorala & S. Jayasuriya, *'Victory in War and Defeat in Peace: Politics and Economics of Post-Conflict Sri Lanka'* (2015) *Asian Economic Papers* 14(3): pp.22-54.

[99] J. Wickramaratne (2014) *Towards Democratic Governance in Sri Lanka: A Constitutional Miscellany* (Colombo: Institute for Constitutional Studies); A. Welikala (Ed.) (2015) *Reforming Sri Lankan Presidentialism: Provenance, Problems and Prospects* (Colombo: Centre for Policy Alternatives).

[100] K.M. De Silva (1986) *Religion, Nationalism, and the State in Modern Sri Lanka* (Florida: University of South Florida); A.J. Wilson (2000) *Sri Lankan Tamil Nationalism* (London: Hurst).

[101] Much earlier analyses were by H. Wriggins (1960) *Ceylon: Dilemmas of a New Nation* (Princeton: Princeton University Press) on linguistic nationalism at the 1956 elections, and R.N. Kearney (1967) *Communalism and Language in the Politics of Ceylon* (Durham: Duke University Press) on communalism in general.

[102] Kearney (1967).

nationalism'[103] or 'separatist nationalism.'[104] On the normative side, however, except for some efforts to promote 'civic nationalism' in contrast to 'ethno-nationalism',[105] the prospects or possibilities for the emergence of more sober or grounded politico-psychological changes in the form of 'cosmopolitanism' has never been contemplated before.

The dramatic political changes that swept the country at the presidential elections in January, and parliamentary elections in August 2015, to re-establish democracy and good governance, however demonstrate a certain maturity of the electorate that could be interpreted as a small but a definitive move towards cosmopolitanism.[106] This was predominantly within a context of a strong parochial discourse and xenophobic movement on nationalism, called *jathika chinthanaya* (nationalist thought), which attempted to preserve not only the status quo after the end of the war on terrorism, but also to move beyond on a further ethno-nationalist direction.[107] After the aforesaid electoral breakthroughs in January and August, the newly formed 'national government' has demonstrated a program of action with certain traits of cosmopolitanism particularly in the areas of foreign affairs and economic policy in recognition of certain global realities.

The purpose of the present chapter therefore is twofold. Considering that cosmopolitanism is a new concept in the Sri Lankan context (although with some past roots), the first part of the chapter would be devoted to elucidating the main facets of that concept relevant to Sri Lankan debates and developments. The second part thereafter is devoted to ascertain the emergence of cosmopolitan trends and tendencies, particularly at the two elections with preliminary empirical evidence based on voting patterns and

---

[103] N. DeVotta (2014) *From Civil War to Soft Authoritarianism: Ethnonationalism and Democratic Regression in Sri Lanka* (New York: Routledge).

[104] A. Bandarage (2009) *The Separatist Conflict in Sri Lanka: Terrorism, Ethnicity, Political Economy* (New York: Routledge).

[105] L. Fernando, 'Sri Lanka's Predicament: Ethno-Nationalism versus Civic-Nationalism', *Asian Tribune*, 25th June 2007; L. Fernando, 'Sri Lanka: On the Question of Nationalism', *Colombo Telegraph*, 13th May 2013.

[106] L. Fernando, 'A Victory for 'Cosmopolitanism' over Narrow Nationalism', *Sri Lanka Guardian*, 29th August 2015.

[107] The pioneer advocate of *jathika chinthanaya* was Gunadasa Amarasekara, a popular fictionist. Later the main ideology became developed by Nalin de Silva (a professor) whose pioneer sketch of this ideology was in *Mage Lokaya* (My World) in 1986. See also, K. Senaratne, 'Jathika Chinthanaya and the Executive Presidency' in Welikala (2015): Ch.16.

electoral demography.

Concept of Cosmopolitanism

Historically speaking, the concept of cosmopolitanism does not belong to one writer or school of thought. It has been used widely and diffusedly throughout centuries and only in recent times has a certain crystallization of the concept emerged both as recognition of 'globalization' and also as a rational critique of it.[108] It is undoubtedly a concept counter to 'narrow nationalism' in the internal dimension, which also deviates from crude globalization on the external frontier.[109] The term, which might still not be very popular or attractive in everyday political parlance, nevertheless is useful as a model of applied theory in visualizing or analyzing certain political trends and recent changes.

Two Thinkers

It is customary to contrast two thinkers, one ancient and the other modern, Diogenes (404-323 BCE) and Emmanuel Kant (1724-1804), to elucidate the evolution of the concept from an individual notion to a much broader social conception. However, it should be noted that the ancient Stoics advocated a similar idea to Kant during the Greek and Roman periods, although this became somewhat tainted with Cicero's advocacy of the 'Empire.' The Stoic advocacy of the notion was as a 'cosmic community', which transcends one's national boundary especially in terms of justice, peace, and equality. This is the same meaning today.

Diogenes of Sinope, however, is considered the originator of the concept, or the term he used: *Kosmopolites* (citizens of the world). He was famous for carrying his daytime lamp as if to find the 'honest man' in the world. Since then cosmopolitanism has been part of moral philosophy. This Cynic philosopher, Diogenes, used to travel almost everywhere possible in the Mediterranean in his ragged clothes and when he was asked where he came from, he used to answer I am from nowhere, 'I am a citizen of the world.'

---

[108] S. Vertovec & R. Cohen (Eds.) (2002) *Conceiving Cosmopolitanism: Theory, Context, and Practice* (Oxford: Oxford University Press); G. Delanty (2009) *The Cosmopolitan Imagination: The Renewal of Critical Social Theory* (Cambridge: Cambridge University Press); D. Held (Ed.) (2010) *Cosmopolitanism: Ideals, Realities & Deficits* (Cambridge: Polity Press); G. Delanty (Ed.) (2012) *Routledge Handbook of Cosmopolitanism Studies* (New York: Routledge).

[109] G. Delanty, *'Nationalism and Cosmopolitanism: The Paradox of Modernity'* in G. Delanty & K. Kumar (Eds.) (2006) *The Sage Handbook of Nations and Nationalism* (London: Sage).

His cosmopolitanism was thus eccentric, rootless, or represented extreme individualism, and might not be good for anyone today. This has been one criticism against cosmopolitanism even thereafter. Jean-Jacque Rousseau once said cosmopolitans argue that 'they love everyone, in order to have the right to love no one.'[110]

The enlightened modern philosopher, Emmanuel Kant, in the late eighteenth century was different. He turned cosmopolitanism on its feet. Therefore, the modern political conception of cosmopolitanism traces its origins to Kant and not to Diogenes. Kant's conception of a cosmopolitan is not as the rootless traveler who picks cultural titbits from different countries. It is an enlightened attitude and a 'world outlook' towards plurality, tolerance, multiculturalism, and co-existence. As Pauline Kleingeld explained:

Instead, on Kant's view, cosmopolitanism is an attitude taken up in action: an attitude of recognition, respect, openness, interest, beneficence and concern towards other human individuals, cultures and peoples as members of one global community.[111]

Kant was not a person who had travelled much or travelled at all. He lived in his hometown Konigsberg, Germany, most of the time. With its seaport, university, government offices, and international trade, he believed that he could easily connect with different languages, religions, and cultures, broaden his knowledge and be part of a 'common humanity.' This does not however deny the merit of travelling for the benefit of experience, knowledge or world outlook. The point is that Kant's cosmopolitanism was not rootles or unconcern for one's own culture or upbringing. Even Kant believed that cosmopolitans can or ought to be 'good patriots.'

The Kantian View

Kant developed cosmopolitanism beyond a mere moral philosophy. In that effort the concept came closer the modern political realities or political realism. It should be noted that he was not the only thinker who advocated cosmopolitanism during his time. Three facets of cosmopolitanism that Kant talked about were political, economic, and cultural. Moreover, he was the first person to develop some clear notions of international institutional

---

[110]Although Rousseau criticised cosmopolitanism of Diogenes' type, he was an advocate of 'civic patriotism' and not 'ethnic patriotism.'

[111] P. Kleingeld (2012) *Kant and Cosmopolitanism: The Philosophical Ideal of World Citizenship* (Cambridge: Cambridge University Press): p. 1.

arrangements within which cosmopolitanism could exist and thrive. The relevance of these ideas loom large today in the context of international obligations of countries and individuals in respect of universal human rights and international justice. Recent debates and changes in Sri Lanka could also be viewed in this light. According to this view, the fate of individuals particularly in the realm of human rights in a country is beyond the formal jurisdiction of that country and is a concern of the global community at large. The concept of 'responsibility to protect' (R2P), recognized by the UN, emerges from that premise.[112]

As in the case of any other philosophy, there are extremes even in the case of cosmopolitanism. The value of the Kantian conceptualization is the avoidance of these extremes. Taking the Cynic notion of cosmopolitanism, detractors always argued about the seeming contradiction between the notion of 'world citizen' and the 'citizen of a country.' According to the Kantian view, these are two dimensions of the same citizenship, emerging from common humanity, the correlation of which would be positive given the way both national actors and the international players interact with each other. According to Kant, the ideal of correlation that could happen is not through a 'world state' but a voluntary federation or a league of nations. In these views, he undoubtedly presaged the formation of the League of Nations (1920) and later the United Nations (1945). Kant was a defender of the plurality of states and not the other way round.

Although there were traces of a racial theory in Kant's early writings,[113] these racial hierarchical views became modified or abandoned later in the 1790s, and he was a firm advocate of cultural plurality in the world, colonial parts of the globe included. Kant held a theory of rights and in the same vein he defended a right to cosmopolitanism. It incorporated a 'right to hospitality' applied to migrants, refugees, and asylum seekers, or similar groups who need assistance from other states or the international community then or today.

Kant is one who extended cosmopolitanism to embrace international trade. It is often viewed as 'free-market cosmopolitanism'. However, even during his time, free-market cosmopolitanism fundamentally differed from free-market liberalism or today's neo-liberalism. He brought the notion of 'economic justice' to the notion of free-market cosmopolitanism. It was his view that international trade promotes peace and perpetual peace. He was

---

[112] G. Evans (2008) *Responsibility to Protect: Ending Mass Atrocity Crimes Once and for All* (Washington: Brookings Institution Press).

[113] Kleingeld (2012).

not advocating unbridled free trade. As Pauline Kleingeld showed,

... Kant's legal and political theory (especially his republicanism, his theory of property, and his defense of state-funded poverty relief) implies that trade should first of all be just, and that it can be 'free' trade only within the bounds of justice.[114]

A brief look at Kant's *Perpetual Peace* (1795) might be the best way to sum up his views on cosmopolitanism.[115] Although his focus was mainly on world peace, his propositions are equally valid for peace within a country like Sri Lanka. Kant was not talking about any kind of peace or temporary peace but perpetual peace. To him, no peace is everlasting unless underlying causes of war or violence are addressed. Given the human inclination for aggression and violence, he opined, perpetual peace also require strict rules and laws based on justice. In a world context, as he said, unless laws are based on addressing the issues of global citizens and their rights, no peace or stability could be achieved in a perpetual manner. World law (or cosmopolitan law) should not merely be the laws between states, but the laws of or for the global citizens. In this respect, he advocated a new vision for international law. The same goes for the laws within states, whether fundamental (constitutional) law or ordinary law. They should address the needs and aspirations of the citizens. This applies in assessing the constitutional reforms in Sri Lanka including the Nineteenth Amendment and future constitution-making.

Cosmopolitanism Studies

It is customary to consider the period since the French Revolution (1789) as the age of nationalism.[116] Kant was an exception or aberration to this period. Within this wave of strong nationalism, notions of cosmopolitanism became submerged if not completely disappeared at least until the end of the Second World War. Marxism was another philosophy which tried to counter nationalism through internationalism, but its many advocates have succumbed to nationalism through various pretexts.[117] It is only recently

---

[114] Ibid: 8.

[115] See J. Bohman & M. Lutz-Bachmann (Eds.) (1997) *Perpetual Peace: Essays on Kant's Cosmopolitan Ideal* (Massachusetts: MIT Press).

[116] H. Kohn (1944) *The Idea of Nationalism: The Study of Its Origins and Background* (New York: The Macmillan Publishers); E.J. Hobsbawm (1990) *Nations and Nationalism since 1780: Programme, Myth, Reality* (Cambridge: Cambridge University Press).

[117] Apart from Marx's famous but often mistaken dictum that 'workers have no

that academic Marxism has been in a position to influence the revival of contemporary cosmopolitanism. There were sincere attempts to prophecy the demise of nationalism after the end of the war by academics like Elie Kedourie,[118] but the attempt became submerged thereafter within the euphoria about nationalism, and much worse, ethnonationalism. But ethnonationalism was not even nationalism proper but its decomposition. It was Kedourie's view that 'for an academic to offer sympathy for nationalism is virtually impertinent.' His failure or weakness perhaps was in not looking for alternatives. It is in this context that the value of increased academic interest in cosmopolitanism studies could be appreciated. These studies are not new but old as we have outlined. Therefore it is also independent from recent global studies or globalization studies. As a normative philosophy, the value of cosmopolitan studies has enlarged nevertheless because of globalization. As Gerard Delanty has argued, "The world may be becoming more and more globally linked by powerful global forces, but this does not make the world more cosmopolitan."[119]Therefore, in the broadest meaning of the term, cosmopolitanism is about broadening the moral, social, cultural and political horizons of people, leaders, and organizations beyond their close confines. It also means an attitude of openness as opposed to closure within and outside a country. It is primarily about going beyond the 'iron cage' of nationalism, whether the country is socialist or capitalist.

There are two major reasons why the concept and philosophy of cosmopolitanism has become crucially important since the last decade of the twentieth century. First is globalization, which has created enormous space for cosmopolitanism in whatever variety you speak of the concept. Technological integration of the world has become the infrastructure through which cosmopolitanism is and can be promoted. If cosmopolitanism is not a natural outcome of globalization, it has become an imperative because of the threats associated with globalization. Globalization has even produced ideas rejecting cosmopolitanism or calling for a new form of cosmopolitanism. The call is for global citizens without states.[120] However, the main theorists of cosmopolitanism and more realist

---

nationality,' his main thesis was arguing against Friedrich List's narrow analysis of the 'national system of political' economy: G. Achcar (2013) *Marxism, Orientalism, Cosmopolitanism* (London: Saqi Books). Marx advocated a world outlook and analysis.

[118] E. Kedourie (1960) *Nationalism* (London: Hutchinson).

[119] Delanty (2012): p. 2.

[120] L. Trepanier & K. Habib (Eds.) (2011) *Cosmopolitanism in the Age of Globalization: Citizens without States* (Kentucky: The University Press of Kentucky).

academics have held the fort. There is no rejection of the state in contemporary cosmopolitanism. Jurgen Habermas has come with 'constitutional patriotism' and Ulrich Beck even with 'cosmopolitan nationalism.' Delanty's conception is 'critical cosmopolitanism.'[121]

Second is the collapse of communism. Developments in this sphere have been bizarre and contradictory. Considering the nature of socialist and communist ideologies, one could have assumed that these countries were favorable to cosmopolitanism. Unfortunately, that was not the case. In the case of some Eastern European countries, some form of cosmopolitanism was applied, although selectively.[122] However, this was not the case in the Soviet Union, and even now, the countries of the former union have not been able to overcome the situation completely. Particularly during the Stalinist period and even thereafter, those who professed any form of free cosmopolitanism, except a limited form of regime sanctioned 'international solidarity,' were considered traitors or 'enemies of communism.' This is still the case in North Korea or even the much economically opened up China. Only Cuba shows clear signs of deviating from such a closed situation. Although the collapse of communism opened up space and opportunities for cosmopolitanism, the actual developments have still not taken place in many countries.

There are many other reasons why cosmopolitanism has become important today. Apart from its utility in countering narrow nationalism, cosmopolitanism has become important as a theoretical framework in understanding many social changes in our midst in Sri Lanka or overseas. As this is being written, thousands and thousands of refugees are fleeing the Syrian crisis and are arriving in Europe, crossing difficult borders seeking 'cosmopolitan hospitality.' Tracing social changes favorable to cosmopolitanism since the early 1990s, Delanty maintained that they are linked up with the "expansion of democracy and the extension of the space for the political."[123] Some of the other developments that he traced were the end of Apartheid, Tiananmen Square upheavals, and democracy movements in the Arab world. There are many others with him who have also acknowledged the importance of the two hundredth anniversary of Kant's 1795 work *Perpetual Peace* in 1995 as an important landmark in the revival of cosmopolitanism. Delanty also noted the following.

---

[121] Delanty (2012): pp. 38-46.

[122] U. Ziemer & S. Roberts (Eds.) (2013) *Eastern European Diasporas, Migration and Cosmopolitanism* (New York: Routledge): p.7.

[123] Delanty (2012): p. 3.

The 1990s were marked not only by such major political events of global significance, but in addition by the arrival of the internet and an epochal revolution in communication technologies which led not only to the transformation of everyday life and politics but capitalism too. The sense of epochal change was enhanced with a sense of a new millennium.[124]

It is on the basis of the above theoretical and conceptual premises, although not comprehensive by any means, that an attempt would be made in the next part of this chapter to understand the recent political changes in Sri Lanka in terms of cosmopolitanism and/or moving away from narrow nationalism.

The Challenge of Change

The interpretation of political change at the two recent elections, in January and August 2015, is the main focus of this second part of the chapter from the point of view of cosmopolitanism that I have outlined above. The dramatic character of this change was signified by the ousting of the leader, the former President Mahinda Rajapaksa, who in fact won the war against 'separatism and terrorism' just six years back in 2009,[125] and therefore the change could safely be interpreted as a – small nevertheless significant – move away from strong ethnonationalism towards a desirable form of cosmopolitanism. The reason or the justification to interpret the election results as a move away from strong ethnonationalism is the fact that the former President Rajapaksa contested both the presidential elections in January and the parliamentary elections in August primarily on the basis of an ethnonationalist election platform.

As far as I am aware, so far, there are no empirical studies conducted on the correlation between the emergence of cosmopolitan trends and electoral or regime change in countries where previously politics were dominated by parochial regimes and narrow nationalism. However, recently Miyase Christensen and André Jansson noted, "Iranian national elections of 2009, the Occupy Movement and the Arab Spring, taken together, have opened up a cosmopolitan space of global debates through popular communication networks."[126] Their focus in discussing the cosmopolitan trends is in relation to the media. It is on the same vein that Lilie Chouliaraki discussed

---

[124] Ibid.

[125] C.A. Chandraprema (2012) *Gota's War* (Colombo: Ranjan Wijeratne Foundation).

[126] M. Christensen & A. Jansson (2015) *Cosmopolitanism and the Media: Cartographies of Change* (New York: Palgrave): p.5.

two case studies, the Haiti earthquake and the Egyptian uprising.[127] Of course the role of the new media or more particularly social media was conspicuous in electoral change, generating cosmopolitan orientations among the voters in Sri Lanka.[128] However, the present interpretation goes beyond this and analyses some important glimpses of voter behavior and changing electoral demography in Sri Lanka in analyzing electoral change and the emergence of cosmopolitan trends.

In addition to the electoral change, accompanied by majority-minority alliances, civil society activities and movements of professional groups, there have emerged certain notions, propositions, and policies that could be associated with some form cosmopolitanism. A major issue at the presidential elections in January for example was 'good governance' or 'compassionate government' (*maithri palanayak*). This was contrasted to the then prevailing rule, which was criticized as authoritarian, corrupt, and nepotistic. The abolition or a fundamental modification of the executive presidential system was promised and it was put into practice, whatever the weaknesses or deficiencies, through the Nineteenth Amendment to the Constitution under the new minority government in April 2015. A most important aspect of the Nineteenth Amendment was the reinstatement of the Constitutional Council and the independent commissions which could give a cosmopolitan orientation to the state administration and structures, drawing the best talent from all communities in society.

At the parliamentary elections in August, the leading coalition, the United National Front for Good Governance (UNFGG), declared a policy of 'Social Market Economy' for the first time in the country. If this is implemented properly, it would be a major boost to cosmopolitanism. Most importantly, the foreign policy orientation has shifted significantly from an anti-Western and anti-UN posture to cooperation and constructive collaboration. This has become very clear from the current government's position at the UN Human Rights Council (2015) in contrast to the

---

[127] L. Chouliaraki & B. Blaagaard (Eds.) (2014) *Cosmopolitanism and the New News Media* (New York: Routledge): Ch.8. It is interesting to note the emergence of a formative type of cosmopolitan solidarity in Sri Lanka during the Asian Tsunami in December 2004. Facing natural calamity, people, transcending ethnic and other barriers, got together. However, this trend did not last long. But the experiences seem to be absorbed by the youth.

[128] One important study in this direction is by N. Gunawardene, '*Sri Lankan Parliamentary Election 2015: How Did Social Media Make A Difference?*', *Groundviews*, 3rd September 2015.

previous postures of the previous government. There are many other policy shifts that could be considered conducive to future cosmopolitanism, but all cannot be discussed within the scope of this section.

Cosmopolitan Electoral Change

The January presidential elections might prove to be a watershed in Sri Lankan political history in recent times. It is called a 'silent revolution' or a 'democratic revolution.' It was 'silent' because it eventuated through the ballot box unlike the Arab Spring. It was a 'democratic revolution' because it managed to oust the incumbent President who was authoritarian and at least undemocratic. He was contesting for an unprecedented third term, after changing the constitution to that effect through dubious means. If he managed to win the elections, the form of Sri Lankan politics would have taken a disastrous path.

At the presidential elections in January when he was defeated, Rajapaksa received only 47.6 per cent of the national vote, whereas his vote at the previous presidential elections in 2010 was 57.9 per cent. This was a 10 per cent swing in percentage terms within less than five years. In contrast, the common opposition candidate and the present President, Maithripala Sirisena, received 51.3 per cent for a comfortable victory whereas the previous opposition candidate in 2010, Sarath Fonseka, received only 40.1 per cent of the national vote. The increase was approximately 11.2 per cent.

More significant was the swing of votes at the parliamentary elections in August from the presidential elections in January. At the parliamentary elections, Rajapaksa contested again as a kind of unofficial prime ministerial candidate. However, his party, the United Peoples Freedom Front (UPFA), with considerable sections now opposing his politics, received only 42.3 per cent of the votes. This was a decrease of 5.3 per cent within seven months. The pre-January 2015 opposition and the interim government (UNFGG) between January and August 2015 received 45.7 per cent. This was also a decrease of 5.7 per cent, as two main constitutive parties of the common opposition in the presidential election, the Tamil National Alliance (TNA) (4.6 per cent) and the Janatha Vimukthi Peramuna (JVP) (4.8 per cent), as well as other smaller parties, contested the parliamentary elections separately. However, when taken together, it was an improvement of 3.8 per cent within seven months.

It is on record that Mahinda Rajapaksa attributed his defeat at the presidential elections to the Tamil vote and was hopeful of winning the parliamentary elections on the basis of the Sinhalese vote in the South. That was the case if only judged by the attendance at his public rallies. But that did not happen. As Nirupama Subramanian reported in *The Indian Express* (19th August 2015), after the last campaign meeting, Rajapaksa had predicted the following:

In almost every district in southern Sri Lanka, I won the presidential election. Sirisena won only because he got the minority votes from Tamils in the North. But this is not a presidential election. This is different. We will win all those districts in this election again and get a majority.

It is true that the Tamil vote particularly in the North and the East was decisive at the last presidential elections. They overwhelmingly voted for the moderate common candidate Maithripala Sirisena. It is interesting to note the voting behavior of those Tamil voters as shown in Table 1 in the last three presidential elections: 2005, 2010 and 2015. The table gives percentages of votes in five Northern and Eastern districts for the seemingly moderate Sinhala candidates, Ranil Wickremesinghe, Sarath Fonseka, and Maithripala Sirisena respectively at the three elections. In all these elections, Rajapaksa contested. The candidates are denoted by their initials as MR (Rajapaksa), RW (Wickremesinghe), SF (Fonseka), and MS (Sirisena).

Table 1: Voter Behavior at Presidential Elections in North and East (Districts)

District	2005			2010			2015		
	Turnout	MR	RW	Turnout	MR	SF	Turnout	MR	MS
Jaffna	1.21	25.00	70.20	25.66	24.75	63.84	66.28	21.85	74.42
Vanni	34.30	20.36	77.89	40.33	27.31	66.86	72.57	19.07	78.47
Batticaloa	48.51	18.87	79.51	64.83	26.27	68.93	70.93	16.22	81.62
Digamadu.	72.70	42.88	55.81	73.54	47.92	49.94	77.39	33.82	65.22
Trinco.	72.70	37.04	61.33	68.22	43.04	54.09	76.76	26.67	71.84

Source: Department of Elections

As the above table shows those voters have preferred a moderate candidate (WR, SF or MS) at all three elections. That is what the percentages show for RW (2005), SF (2010) and MS (2015). At the last elections, MS won 74.42, 78.47, and 81.62 per cent of vote in the three districts of Jaffna, Vanni, and Batticaloa respectively. Even MR could not win such a percentage in his home turf, Hambantota in the South, even at the 2010 elections, which was 67.21 per cent in 2010 and 63.02 per cent at the last elections. The most important factor is the voter turnouts at these elections, in respect of voting for the moderate candidates.

At 2005 elections, there was extreme polarization between the two communities or the North and the South. There was a pronounced boycott in the North (particularly in Jaffna and Vanni) engineered by the Liberation Tigers of Tamil Eelam (LTTE). The overwhelming demand at that time was a 'separate state' and not ethnic accommodation. The voter turnout was extremely low: mere 1.21 per cent in Jaffna and 34.30 per cent in Vanni. It is true that the voters were prevented by coercion. However, even at the 2010 elections, the voter turnouts were 25.66 and 40.33 per cent in the respective two districts. What this voter behavior shows is moderation, and an increasing 'cosmopolitan' disposition moving away from the extremism that was evident in 2005. Judging by these election results, there has been a clear desire and willingness on the part of the Northern Tamils in the country for ethnic accommodation at the last elections, both presidential and parliamentary, which have brought political change to the country.

Other Factors

The electoral behavior of the other minorities, particularly the Muslims and the Hill Country Tamils, has been different. Judging by the positions of the Sri Lanka Muslim Congress (SLMC) and the Ceylon Workers Congress (CWC), two main parties of the two communities respectively, what could be seen until lately is the willingness for political accommodation with the Sinhalese majority or the ruling party UPFA. Although both parties supported the moderate candidate, Wickremesinghe, at the 2005 presidential elections, both parties were willing to work with Rajapaksa after his victory in 2005, even at the risk of losing rank and file support. This was one reason for various splits and splinters from both parties. However the situation was unviable particularly for the SLMC and the Muslim community by the time of the 2015 elections. There had been major attacks on religious places of the Muslim community since 2013. Similarly, there were attacks on evangelical Christian places of congregation during the same period. Therefore, apart from the Tamils concentrated in the Northern and some parts of the Eastern Province, the other dispersed sections of the Tamils (originally Northern or Hill country), the Muslims, and even the Christians were catalysts in bringing about electoral change both at the presidential and parliamentary elections.

There are other researchers who have employed regression analysis to examine voter behavior between 2010 and 2015 presidential elections[129]. They have examined factors that contributed to the dramatic change in the

---

[129] Athukorala & Jayasuriya (2015).

'Mahinda Rajapaksa Margin' (MRM) between the two elections and found that inter-district differences in the 'share of all minorities' played a key role, other than what we have discussed in Table 1 for the Northern and the Eastern districts. They have shown that the 'share of all ethnic minorities' combined with the 'share of urban population' in an electoral district/province have affected the MRM to drop.[130] Two other relevant variables, which the authors could have included in this regression analysis, are the 'religious minorities' (i.e. Christians) and the 'share of youth' in the electoral demography.

By the general elections in August, however, it became clear that even where the 'share of all minorities' has been absent or low, the MRM has dropped (i.e. Polonnaruwa or even Moneragala). This may be due to the 'youth element' or leadership factors. This is also where the cosmopolitan effect has emerged in the case of the Sinhala majority districts. It has been my conviction that urbanization and modern youth play a major role in cosmopolitanism in any country and particularly in Sri Lanka. This is without a distinction as to ethnicity or religion. They are the people who are largely influenced by the 'new news media' discussed in Chouliaraki and Blaagaard (2014).[131] They are equipped with the 'social media' devices that Nalaka Gunawardene talked about in Sri Lanka this year.[132] Between 2010 and 2015, there has been nearly a million newly registered voters, all youth. The percentage of population and thus probably the percentage of voters between 18 years and 25 is nearly 15 per cent with a decisive say in an election. They may remain dormant without leadership particularly in rural areas. But when they are given leadership or opportunity they become activated. That is what was demonstrated in the August general elections. Table 2 shows the voter shift between the 2010 and 2015 parliamentary elections in respect of the two main contending parties/coalitions on a percentage basis in districts other than in the North and East. This is in a way the cosmopolitan shift.

---

[130] It may also be useful to undertake this analysis at the electorate level where the variations in these variables would be more conspicuous.

[131] Chouliaraki & Blaagaard (2014).

[132] Gunawardene (2015).

Table 2: Voter Preference at Parliamentary Elections in Districts (Other than North and East)

	UNP/UNFGG			UPFA		
	2010	2015	% Change	2010	2015	% Change
Central Province						
Kandy	34.48	55.57	+21.09	60.77	38.98	-21.79
Matale	28.47	49.84	+21.37	66.96	45.54	-21.42
Nuwaraeliya	36.39	59.01	+22.62	56.01	37.98	-18.03
Southern Province						
Galle	26.03	42.48	+16.45	66.17	50.07	-16.10
Matara	27.81	39.08	+11.27	65.31	52.44	-12.67
Hambantota	29.86	35.65	+5.79	62.87	53.84	-9.03
Western Province						
Colombo	36.17	53.00	+16.83	51.19	39.21	-11.98
Gampaha	28.67	47.13	+18.46	63.37	44.92	-18.45
Kalutara	28.32	44.47	+16.15	63.68	48.56	-15.12
North-Western						
Kurunegala	31.78	45.85	+14.07	63.84	49.26	-14.58
Puttalam	31.36	50.40	+19.04	64.83	42.83	-22.00
North-Central Province						
Anuradhapura	24.17	44.82	+20.65	66.52	48.35	-18.17
Polonnaruwa	26.67	50.26	+23.59	69.22	43.63	-25.59
Sabaragamuwa Province						
Ratnapura	28.21	44.94	+16.73	68.86	51.19	-17.77
Kegalle	28.95	49.52	+20.57	66.89	45.47	-21.42
Uva Province						
Badulla	32.28	54.76	+22.48	58.25	37.97	-20.28
Moneragala	18.12	41.97	+23.85	75.64	52.53	-23.11
National	29.34	45.66	+16.32	60.33	42.38	-17.95

Source: Department of Elections and Wikipedia. Note that figures under 'National' include North and East.

As this table shows, the overall shift towards the UNP/UNFGG has been +23.85 per cent and the drop of MRM -23.11 per cent. The most significant shifts have taken place in districts where the 'share of minorities' or the 'multicultural dimension' is high. The Central Province, and its three districts – Nuwara Eliya (+22.62), Matale (+21.37) and Kandy (+21.09) – stand prominent. In this province, taken as an example, the share of the Muslims and the Hill Country Tamils stands high, but without a major shift among the Sinhalese, the above result could not have been possible.[133]

Another significant factor in the cosmopolitan shift in elections is the 'share of urbanization.' The count of urbanization in Sri Lanka is not very sophisticated. The urban population is still considered 18.4 per cent, counted on the basis of the population in municipal and urban council areas. Even if this methodology is acceptable, it has been an extremely slow and cumbersome process to upgrade divisional (rural) councils to urban councils or municipal councils. There are 23 municipal councils and 41 urban councils at present. If we take the municipal council areas as an example, all cannot be considered congruent with old electorates although names are the same.[134] For example, the Colombo Municipal Council area covers several electorates. However, it is interesting to note that out of 23 municipal council areas, the voting in 14 areas went significantly in favor of the UNFGG, and the UPFA could win only 6 areas at the last general elections in August. When it came to the urban council areas, the congruence between a parliamentary electorate and a local government area is complicated. However, most of the urban council areas out of 41 were located within the districts, which were won by the UNFGG.

Having said the above, the 'cosmopolitanism' of rural voters should not be underestimated. After all, Sri Lanka is a small country with high connectivity. As the above table shows, the highest drop of the MRM was in Polonnaruwa (-25.59) and then came Moneragala (-23.11), although the latter district could not be won by the UNFGG. What this shift signifies is the leadership factor, and at elections, the campaign factor countering parochial nationalism.

There were other cosmopolitan trends discernible at the parliamentary elections. For example, the extremist political parties could not get much of a foothold whether in the South or the North. The political party of the infamous Bodu Bala Sena (Buddhist Force Army), the Bodu Jana Peramuna (BJP), contested 16 districts but obtained only 20,377 votes, mere 0.18 per cent of the total polled. The fate of the Tamil National People's Front (TNPF) was very much similar, obtaining only 18,644 votes in Jaffna and

---

[133]This chapter does not attempt to analyse all the important figures in the table for want of space.

[134]The municipal council areas are: Colombo, Dehiwala-Mt. Lavinia, Kotte, Kaduwela, Moratuwa, Negombo, Gampaha, Kurunegala, Kandy, Matale, Dambulla, Nuwara Eliya, Badulla, Bandarawela, Galle, Matara, Hambantota, Ratnapura, Anuradhapura, Jaffna, Batticaloa, Kalmunai, and Akkairapattu.

0.17 per cent altogether. The UNFGG managed to win one seat each in Jaffna and Vanni districts showing also a trend of cosmopolitanism among the overwhelmingly Tamil voters, some of whom favoring national parties who assure minority rights.

Conclusion

There were two purposes to the present chapter, one theoretical and the other empirical or practical. The first part of the chapter outlined cosmopolitanism as a concept and a social philosophy, or one might even say an ideology, which could supply a viable alternative to narrow nationalism or ethnonationalism in the case of Sri Lanka or any other country. The second part of the chapter was based on the observation that cosmopolitanism is also a social phenomenon that might appear or disappear, like any other phenomenon, and that it has appeared at the last two elections in January and August in bringing desirable political change and democracy to the country. There have been emerging synergies between cosmopolitanism, democracy, and good governance. The empirical evidence related to the two elections were analyzed to ascertain this cosmopolitan trend within the limits of this short chapter.

When cosmopolitanism is understood in that twin manner, it is an obvious conclusion to say that cosmopolitanism can be promoted both as a social philosophy or a public policy on the one hand, and as a political culture (with values and attitudes) through education with desirable social or electoral behavior on the other hand. It is also evident that the social foundations of cosmopolitanism could be further expanded and strengthened through measures such as urbanization, promotion of cultural integration of different communities, and technological advancements in communication. It is important to note that what appeared as an urban phenomenon with minority input at the presidential elections expanded into the rural areas at the general elections. Political leadership (i.e., President Sirisena, Prime Minister Wickremesinghe and former President Kumaratunga) and organizational factors (i.e., the UNFGG) in promoting cosmopolitanism might be the most decisive factors in this link at present and in the future. The modern youth equipped with information technology undoubtedly played (and would play) a decisive role in this transition both in the urban and rural areas.

(This chapter was previously published under the title "Cosmopolitanism as a Framework for Understanding Recent Political Change in Sri Lanka" in Asanga Welikala (Ed), *The Nineteenth Amendment to the Constitution*)

15
Achieving Balanced Regional Development through Devolution

"...those ethnic-linguistic features so prominent in the ideologies of nationalism have always been secondary to the material factors of uneven development." - Tom Nairn

Whatever the weaknesses of the 13th Amendment or devolution in the present constitution, there is a clear socio-economic philosophy behind it, for the benefit of the people living in the provinces. That is the objective of 'balanced regional development' which can hardly be achieved under a complete unitary state. This is something which needs to be carried forward and strengthened in a new constitution.

It is generally accepted that 'uneven development' is one underlying reason for many of the ethnic and other social conflicts in the world. This is similar to the thesis put forward by Tom Nairn in his *'Break-up of Britain'* in 1977. Youth unrest, rebellions and thereafter armed struggles developed both in the South and in the North primarily in the country's poor and underdeveloped provinces. The acceptance of this fact is not about economic determinism or rejection of other political factors such as the dreadful ethnic discrimination/suppression in the case of the civil war in the North/East, but placing those conflicts in a broader socio-economic background.

Sri Lanka's constitution making is perennially weak in conceptualizing the principles behind institutions, structures, authorities and resultant powers in the governing system. They are mostly dry and boring legal documents. If they refer to concepts at all, they are mostly abstract in nature or repetition of what appears in text books (e.g. people's sovereignty). The 13th Amendment is also the same in most of its formulations. However, there are some gems among the stones. 'Balanced regional development' undoubtedly is one of those gems.

Objective of Balanced Development

Although the 'balanced regional development' is tagged to the Finance Commission (FC) in the 13th Amendment, its objective can be considered one of the main pillars of devolution in general. It is not clear whether the provincial councils or the central government ever took this objective into proper account. It was always relegated to the FC and considered just as a formula for financial allocation, yet within the strictures of the Treasury. What the Article 154 (R) (5) says on 'balanced regional development' is the following.

"(5) The Commission shall formulate such principles with the objective of achieving balanced regional development in the country, and shall accordingly take into account -
    (a) the population of each Province;
    (b) the per capita income of each Province;
    (c) the need progressively, to reduce social and economic disparities; and
    (d) the need, progressively, to reduce the difference between the per capita income of each Province and the highest per capita income among the Provinces."

The above is the present (legal) status. Even in the future, it might be advisable to have a truly independent commission to assist the provincial councils and even the central government in formulating 'such principles with the objective of achieving balanced regional development' not only among provinces but also within. There is such a commission in South Africa called the 'Finance and Fiscal Commission.' In the case of Sri Lanka, it might be better to call it the 'Finance and Planning Commission' as there are major planning matters to be sorted out apart from finance and fiscal matters.

However, 'balanced regional development' is primarily a task for the provincial councils and the central government in mutual cooperation, and not for the FC in isolation. The best model for Sri Lanka in this case is 'cooperative devolution.' When you take the population of each province, per capita income, socio-economic disparities, and the 'difference between the per capita income of each province and the highest per capita income among the provinces,' the massive uneven development in Sri Lanka is very clear. What is missing in this inventory might be the 'disparities in natural resources and environmental conditions.' These also have to be taken into account in trying to ameliorate uneven development in the country.

'Uneven development' largely is a product of colonialism and lopsided capitalist development. It is not clear whether the pre-colonial situation was even or balanced. Perhaps not. However, we have more accurate information since the colonial period. It is mainly the Western province that became 'developed' under (British) colonialism and the unitary state. The unitary state, and politics controlled from Colombo, contributed to this debacle. Even though major surpluses were extracted from the tea plantations, the central province remained underdeveloped as the benefits were not distributed to that province or the people.

This was underdevelopment within underdevelopment. In the provinces, although major towns such as Jaffna, Gale, Trincomalee, Nuwara Eliya or Kandy were developed, the purpose was mainly administrative and not socio-economic. This is the trend which has to be reversed, and one of the main ways that could be done is through devolution. Take the one time popular saying in the south, '*kolombata kiri apata kakiri*,' literally meaning 'milk for Colombo and melon for us' or 'everything for Colombo and nothing for us.' There is an undeniable truism in this saying even today.

Obstructing Uneven Development

There has been a very clear 'center-periphery dichotomy' in Sri Lanka both in the economy, and in the socio-political sphere since independence, the Western province dominating. This dichotomy became overwhelming under the open economy after 1977. Let me give some empirical evidence in the following Table (GDP Share by Province, 1990-2015) for the last 25 years.

Table 1: GDP Shares by Province, 1990-2015 (%)

Province	1990	2000	2010	2015
Western	40.2	49.6	45.1	41.2
Central	12.1	10.4	10.0	10.3
Southern	9.5	9.4	10.7	10.4
Northern	4.4	2.2	3.4	3.5
North Western	11.1	10.4	9.4	10.9
North Central	4.8	3.9	4.8	5.4
Uva	8.1	3.9	4.5	5.2
Eastern	4.2	4.5	5.9	6.0
Sabaragamuwa	8.1	6.7	6.3	7.0
Sri Lanka	100.0	100.0	100.0	100.0

Source: Central Bank of Sri Lanka, Annual Reports

According to these figures, the Western province still remains dominant in the economy (41.2), but since the end of the war, some course correction is underway. The GDP share of the province was 40.2 in 1990, but increased during the war, peaking in 2000-2005 period. The figure for 2005 was 50.8 percent. The Eastern province, traditionally called the 'granary of the country,' once contributed 14 percent, but declined under the open economy and then the war.

'Open economy' is a policy that Sri Lanka cannot avoid, but to counter the adverse effects, a 'balanced regional development' is necessary. By 2015, only the Central, the Southern and the North Western provinces could achieve a 10 percent contribution. Among the other provinces, while the North Central (5.4), Uva (5.2), Eastern (6.0) and Sabaragamuva (7.0) struggling above the 5 percent mark, the Northern province is still lagging behind around 3.5 percent, even after the end of the war. Uneven development and regional underdevelopment not only highlight the need for devolution, but emphasizes the requirement for rethinking as to the way it should proceed in the future.

Some Causal Reasons

The argument here is not about having equal share of GDP for all provinces. This is unthinkable given the provincial disparities in population among other factors. The population share of the Western province for example is around 29 percent, and it is natural therefore for that province to achieve a higher share of the GDP also given the fact that physical capital (i.e. infrastructure) and the human capital (i.e. education, health) are comparatively higher. The following Table 2 gives a comparative picture of the population share (2012) and the GDP share (2015) for the provinces.

Table 2: Population (2012) and GDP Share (2015) of Provinces (%)

Province	Population Share	GDP Share	Deviation
Western	28.7	41.2	+22.5
Central	12.6	10.3	-2.3
Southern	12.1	10.4	-1.7
Northern	5.4	3.5	-1.9
North Western	11.7	10.9	-0.8
North Central	6.2	5.4	-0.8
Uva	6.2	5.2	-1.0
Eastern	7.6	6.0	-1.6
Sabaragamuwa	9.5	7.0	-2.5

Source: Census and Central Bank

It is obvious that a province like the North Central or Uva might not achieve a share like the Western. The population shares are different. This applies to the other provinces, and also to the North and the East. However, given the vast areas of land in all these provinces what they can achieve in agricultural production might be immense, if the agriculture is modernized (largely physical capital) and the agricultural labor is better skilled (human capital). It is also too obvious that financial capital does not flow, internal or external (FDI), unless there are sufficient base for physical and particularly human capital in the provinces.

Considering that difference in physical and human capital is the main reasons for uneven share of GDP among different provinces, a major task for devolution would be to bridge these disparities. While reliable data are not available for a proper comparisons, some of these disparities are also visible. When you travel from Colombo to the North (North Central included), East, Uva or the deep-South, you come across underdevelopment, poverty and poor infrastructure facilities. What you might not see visibly are the social or human development conditions. These are the poor conditions particularly in health and education and also gender inequalities.

Sri Lanka Human Development Report 2012 (UNDP) gives a valuable comparison from pages 15 to 19. According to these information, calculated primarily on the district basis, Gampaha, Kalutara and Colombo, stands the highest in that order in the human development index (HDI), while the Northern Province is the lowest as a province. As districts outside the Northern Province, Nuwara Eliya, Batticaloa and Badulla stand the lowest in HDI. As these information also show, the disparities are not only between provinces, but also within provinces, both at the district and divisional levels. That is one reason why the devolution has to go deeper, and into the divisional or local government levels.

There are some welcome developments when the year 2015 is compared with 2014. This however should not be exaggerated considering the progress that needs to be achieved in the future. As the Central Bank reported, the share of the GDP of other provinces (other than the Western) increased from 58.3 in 2014 to 58.8 percent in 2015. All these provinces performed better in 2015 except Uva recording a decline. The Eastern province doubled its growth rate while the North achieving a 12.1 percent growth rate. Both provinces were rising from a lower base, and the growth was in agriculture and not in industries or services.

A Possible Way Out

There are obvious two extremes to be avoided if balanced regional development needs to be achieved in the country through devolution. One is the 'unitary' thinking where the dominant politicians and the bureaucrats believe that regional development can be achieved or projected from Colombo. This can and have happened even under devolution. The other is the emotional political demands or 'separatist' thinking of many minority politicians neglecting the socio-economic factors of the issues involved. Both are self-serving devices on the part of the elitist politicians. Sri Lanka has experimented both, but has failed miserably.

While the initial national economic plans, first the ten year (1956-65) and then the five year (1970-75), geared from Colombo failed to achieve balanced regional development, the 'bull in a china shop' approach of the open economy (since 1977) had been a colossal disaster in this respect. The present predicament is that both the 'unitary' thinking and 'separatism' still dominate the devolution debate as well as its crooked practices. One consequence is the vast disparities in income distribution throughout the country. According to the available figures, the poorest 20 percent of the population receives only 4.5 percent of total household income, while the richest 20 percent receiving 54.1 percent, although the absolute poverty is now comparatively low.

A major reason for this situation is the vastly 'underdeveloped' outer provinces. Despite the immense income inequalities in the Western province itself, the per capita income is 140 percent higher than all the other provinces combined. Thus a major objective of devolution should be 'balanced regional development.' There is nothing particularly wrong in having a 'megapolis' in the West or 'smart cities,' but there should also be 'smart cities' in other provinces as well. In reformulating what appears in Article 154, in clarifying the primary objective/s of devolution, it could be said:

Both the provincial councils and the national government shall formulate such principles with the objective of achieving regional development in the country, with the assistance of a Finance and Planning Commission, and shall accordingly take into account –

the population of each province;

the per capita income of each province;

the level of physical and human capital of each province;

the disparities in natural and environmental conditions between provinces;

the need progressively, to reduce social and economic disparities; and

the need, progressively, to reduce the difference between the per capita income of each province and the highest per capita income among the provinces.

What might be necessary in achieving such a 'balanced regional development' obviously is 'cooperative devolution.' It is also clear that if such an objective is accepted in a new constitution, more research needs to be done particularly in assessing the existing levels of 'physical and human capital' and also quantifiable 'natural and environmental conditions' in and between provinces.

(This is a most recent article published in *The Island*, the *Colombo Telegraph* and the Sri *Lanka Guardian* in August 2016)

16
Civil Society Must Take Over Local Governments

"Freedom consists in the conversion of the State from an organ superimposed on society into one completely subordinated to it." - Karl Marx

As an exemplary gesture in 2006, a former Senior Additional Solicitor General, Srinath Perera, contested a local government council (Boralesgamuwa Urban Council) believing that 'the lack of committed, decent and capable people coming forward' was one of the factors for the deterioration of the local government system. Giving an interview on his extraordinary decision to the '*Sunday Island*' (26 March 2006) he said:

I believe that the overall system [i.e. free education] has allowed me to achieve what I have achieved and I felt a need to give back something in return before I die. I am also aware that there are very few educated people who are willing to enter the fray and for very good reasons too. On the other hand a lot can be done if committed, decent and capable people come forward, especially in local authorities.

His example was an isolated incident which was not emulated or continued thereafter. Instead we have seen rapists, killers, thugs and extortionists getting hold of the power in many local councils with the support of major political parties or party leaders in order to keep their power bases at local and grassroots levels intact. This is a vicious link that needs to be broken.

Importance

The importance of the local government system doesn't need to be overemphasized. It is self- evident. The importance is not only for the democratic pyramid, with 336 local councils at the bottom, but also for economic development and social welfare. The system has ancient inspirational roots in the 'Gam-Sabha' system, modernized and/or substituted during the British period. It is less recognized that the people in the country first learnt about the value of the franchise or the representative democracy through the local government system, however limited, well before the universal franchise was introduced for the State Council in 1931.

Local governments are the public/state institutions closest to the people and their day to day as well as development needs from garbage collection to building approvals through health, sanitation, local roads and environmental protection. When the local government system was reformed in 1987, 'community development' was introduced as a major function also allowing the local councils to get involved in 'enterprises' in partnership with the private sector (PPP).

The tasks of the local government institutions have evolved from purely supplying 'utility services' to at least promoting 'social-development,' although these have not been undertaken in the past, during the dark-days. It is a mindboggling question whether many of our local councilors, former and hoping to contest again have any notion of these important tasks! The country's civil war undoubtedly was a disruptive factor and also an easy excuse. The local government areas also can be considered as economic units or 'developmental zones.' When properly coordinated with the provincial councils and the central government agencies i.e. the Divisional Secretariats, these councils or institutions can potentially deliver a yeoman service for economic and social development. The creation of 'One Stop' shops or offices to supply all the services of the local government, provincial councils and the central government in one vicinity could be the most beneficial for the people. This is about the future and not necessarily the present.

Urgent Need

The pressing need however at present is the holding of the much delayed elections for the local government councils, eliminating the mess created by the last government, and also the present one, in the electoral system. As the new constitution making hopefully is going to look at the electoral system afresh, it is best to conduct the local council elections under the old

PR system, unfortunately with its integral defects. If the government is wise, it can avoid some of the glaring defects quickly or allow the Elections Commission and the Police to enforce the election laws strictly. The Minister's claim that there is 'no old system left' is only rhetoric and not correct. What is absent is a 'new system.' The available 'bits and pieces' in the form of the 2012 Amendment, the 2015 Delimitation Report and even the 2016 Amendment are highly defective and contradictory.

The representative government is not about the numbers or the quantity, but about the quality. What the haphazard reforms have done is to inflate the numbers without much sense. The 2012 delimitation committee has carved out 4,833 wards to elect 5,092 members while the previous number was 4,486. When the 30 percent PR component is added it will be 6,619; and with the 25 percent women representation, the total will be 8,274. This is an increase of the number of councilors by 3,788; equivalent to 85 percent increase. While there is no direct need to increase the number of representatives according to the population growth, this increase is more than the double of the population growth (40%) since 1987 when the PR system was introduced.

There are many other legal ambiguities preventing the elections other than the mess in the half-baked electoral system. The Election Commission has requested the government to rectify them, but unfortunately without any progress. This is another reason why the elections should be held under the 'old' PR system. By enacting a brief amendment to the Local Authorities Elections Ordinance to revoke the past amendments since 2012, this could simply be done. In addition, if a clear limit to election expenditure and a strict prohibition of election violence could be imposed, these can be implemented by the Elections Commission and the Police.

Over Politicization

One of the major problems of the local government system is over politicization. This is also linked to corruption, mismanagement, abuse and inefficiency. Whatever the local councilors do are usually defended by the party hierarchies at the top. This is normally the case when the councilors are aligned with the ruling party. Others may lie low until they get the opportunity, or otherwise they usually crossover. There is another aspect to over politicization. That is the councilors' unwarranted interference in local government administration. The tasks of the councilors are to represent people, debate policy, approve budgets, oversee administration, question when the administrators' make mistakes or slack in duty, and make proposals for new initiatives. Their task is not to interfere in administration.

There is a pressing need in improving quality and the management aspects of local government. This can best be done by adopting and efficiently implementing 'management or business excellence frameworks.' These are not unknown to Sri Lanka, particularly in the private sector, whether it be Malcolm Baldridge (American), European Model (EFQM) or the Australian Framework (ABEF). Sri Lanka possibly can develop its own framework/s. All these to happen, there should be a breakthrough at the next elections. There is no much point in having big party competitions in local councils or for council elections. Much worse is when competitions are conducted purely on national issues. The functions of the local government councils are well defined and limited as explained before. If there is any connection between the national issues and the local ones, that is about the connection between macro policies and micro application. The local elections or competitions should be primarily on local issues, policies and development plans, of course within a national (as well as a global) perspective.

The local elections should not be considered a mere barometer of popularity of national parties i.e. the ruling party verses the opposition. It might not be possible to change this mind-set overnight, but there should be efforts to do so. If the major parties care for democracy in the country, they should allow the local or district party organizations to function properly without controlling them from Colombo or Jaffna. This is relevant not only for the UNP and the SLFP, but also for the parties like the TNA. The need for devolution or decentralization is not only for the state structures, but also for party organizations.

Why Civil Society?

The people however cannot wait until the corrupt political parties or politicians get reorganized. It might never happen. That is why the civil society should take over. It was Karl Marx who once said *"Freedom consists in the conversion of the State from an organ superimposed on society into one completely subordinated to it, and today too, the forms of the State are more free or less free to the extent that they restrict the 'freedom' of the State."*[135] This is about democratic transformation and this could begin from the bottom up, through the local government system. Society in general means a larger entity. The most conscious or the organized section is called the civil society. That is why we talk about the role of the 'civil society' than the society in general in meeting this task in practical terms.

---

[135] Quoted by Perry Anderson (1974), *Lineages of the Absolutist State* (London: Verso), p. 11.

In the present day politics and the representative democracy, there is a contradiction between the state and the civil society. This has been emphasized equally by the socialist as well as the liberal thinkers. This contradiction is also evident between the 'political society' and the civil society. By 'political society' here we mean mainly the status quo or conventional political parties. This contradiction is usually enhanced after an election. Once they get elected, it is the natural tendency of the leaders or the so-called people's representatives to get alienated or distanced themselves from the people and people's aspirations. The reasons are due to their newly acquired closeness to 'power and money.' This is apart from willful treachery to acquire both. This has become abundantly clear after the two democratic elections (did we say 'revolutions'?) last year.

The resolution or mediation of this contradiction should come from the civil society. This is part of the democratic cause. Awareness, vigilance, exposure, pressure and defiance are some of the ways. There are some advantages in doing so in modern times due to advances in information technology, free media and the growing awareness and resolve against injustices, corruption and power abuse. The surest way however is direct intervention. The direct intervention by the civil society.

Conclusion

What I am concluding simply is for the organized civil society or the civil society organizations to take over the local governments. My appeal is for the civil society organizations – of women, youth, professionals, academics, media, artists, trade unions, small businesses, NGOs, citizens and seniors – to contest the local government elections in coordination, with commitment and discipline, and to defeat the UNP and the SLFP. If the SLFP (UPFA), the UNP and the TNA are committed to democracy and good governance, they should allow the civil society organizations to take over LG's at least in certain areas on an experimental basis. It should also be emphasized that if the civil society organizations fail to coordinate themselves, eschew any conflicts, become committed and disciplined, and most importantly fail to select the correct candidates, the result might be worse than the existing political parties.

(This article was published in the *Colombo Telegraph* and the *Sri Lanka Guardian* in April 2016)

17
Two Dimensions of the National Question

"While you are intent upon the cure of one part, you may make worse the malady of the other part." - Thomas More

There have been two clearly discernible dimensions to the 'national question' in Sri Lanka in modern times. By modern times, I mean the period beginning with colonialism particularly under the British (1815) and the awakening of various ethnic communities into national consciousness under capitalism and print capitalism. The first dimension of the national question signified or still signifies the independence from colonialism and after independence (1948), the freedom from post-colonialism or what is perceived as imperialism or outside interference, primarily from the Western hemisphere. This can be termed as the external dimension of the national question. The 'independence,' 'sovereignty' and 'territorial integrity' have been the main demands or slogans of this dimension of the national question while it also could invoke the 'overall right of self-determination' of the country. At times, India has also come into this equation as a challenge or a threatening power.

The second dimension of the national question has been the much vexed problem in the country for the last three decades or even before and the failure to resolve this problem peacefully has been the reason for the war, death and destruction. The second dimension of the national question means the 'Tamil national question' or the national question of the minorities particularly of the Tamils and the Muslims. This is the internal dimension of the national question. As ethnic nations or national groups in society, they rightfully aspire for national equality in many spheres and denial of them has led, on the part of the Tamils, to demand 'autonomy,' 'federalism' (internal self-determination) and 'separation' (external self-determination). The 'self-determination' has been their main slogan or demand in various forms.

In contrast to the peaceful resolution of the first or the external dimension of the national question and independence, the abysmal failure on the part of the political leaders to resolve the internal dimension or the second dimension of the national question is very much conspicuous. This article attempts to highlight the inverse relationship between these two dimensions of the national question with a brief outline of their origins and argues that a creative or a rational balance between the two might be the solution for the country's present deadlock on reconciliation and other issues.

Realty and Exaggeration

National questions are always exaggerated matters, whether external and internal. Humans, unlike the other species of animals, appear to have an incorrigible tendency to 'imagine' and 'exaggerate' the perceived threats and kill each other on those grounds. Sri Lankans perhaps in this respect are par excellence. Then the 'theoreticians' like us come in and complicate matters to the greatest possible extent! In the early fifties, it was the 'communist threat' under the influence of the American propaganda. I recollect, as a child, collecting pamphlets from the Colombo Plan Exhibition depicting the killings and atrocities of the communists in Tibet and in the Soviet Union. Then in the seventies it was the threat of American imperialism influenced by the Vietnam War. Even the Mahavelli project was considered a conspiracy. I remember myself writing a popular pamphlet on the subject by the name of Ranjith Peiris condemning American imperialism. Thereafter came the phobia of 'Indian expansionism,' which was utilized by the JVP to mobilize the cadres for the 1971 uprising.

None of the above was completely unreal but exaggerated. When Sri Lanka was a colony, the independence was a primary necessity and the struggle to achieve that was legitimate. Even after independence, there were colonial strings attached and the attempts to untie them were necessary. But to keep the country and the people under constant tension, often under the rubric of 'patriotism,' exaggerating the perceived external threats do more harm than good for the country and its future. The world is undoubtedly controlled by big powers or 'imperialists' no doubt, but there have been many legal and institutional changes under the UN that makes it possible for Sri Lanka to maintain its independence and necessary sovereignty intact. It is a matter of effective diplomacy.

There is no doubt that Sri Lanka is a country which has treated its minorities quite abysmally with or without the threat of separatism. But the first half of the twentieth century was an example for peaceful coexistence between the different ethnic communities, undoubtedly with frictions, or otherwise the country could not have achieved independence as one country. While there is the dominance of Sinhala (or Buddhist) fundamentalism on the one hand, it is equally true that Tamil nationalism also entertained something similar or at least exclusivist traits from the beginning. This is no surprise given the underdeveloped nature of the economy and the social formations where ethno-nationalism became predominant instead of civic nationalism. A major difference between the two, that needs to be taken into proper consideration, however, is that one is the majority (dominant) and the other is the minority.

Once a country has gone through a long period of ethno-nationalism, it is difficult to forge civic nationalism even if the economic conditions change in favor of the latter like perhaps at present. The attempts to create 'civic nationalism' or integration by force would be a catastrophic failure with disastrous consequences. When it is attempted without the consent of the minority, the Tamils or the Muslims, it amounts to forceful assimilation. This is exactly what is attempted and happening today.

Inverse Relationship

In a country like Sri Lanka, compromises are necessary in 'nation building,' in addition to ensuring democracy and development. Bigotry or extremism will not work. A necessary compromise is in between the two dimensions of the national question, the external and the internal. There are opposite forces governing these two dimensions, centripetal and centrifugal. This is in addition as well as in conjunction with the extreme Sinhala nationalism and the extreme Tamil nationalism. A compromise, a balance or equilibrium is needed because the relations are opposite and inverse.

Sinhala nationalism or centripetal forces have been the determining forces in Sri Lanka particularly after independence until they came to a breaking point in the eighties resisted by Tamil nationalism with violence. Although there was some logic in respect of 'recolonization,' the assertion of the external dimension was taken to an extreme end to the detriment of the internal dimension or the minority question. The Sinhala only official language policy and the 1972 Constitution are two major examples.

Absolute 'sovereignty,' 'unitary state' and 'territorial integrity' were the main assertions while the outright rejection of autonomy, devolution or federalism for the minority communities was the major implication. What became revealed was the inherent inverse relationship between the two dimensions. When one is overtly asserted, the other is sweepingly undermined.

It was after the Indian (external) intervention that an uneasy compromise was built into the constitution in 1987 through the 13th Amendment. However this half-hearted compromise could not by now appease the separatist movement. Even the peace efforts by the external intervention could not rectify the situation thereafter. The Norwegian sponsored Ceasefire Agreement (CFA) in fact on the other hand undermined the external dimension of the national question of sovereignty and territorial integrity of the country. At least that is the way it was perceived. Apart from terrorism, this is one reason for the military onslaught against the LTTE in 2006-09. Now after three years of the end of the war, the pendulum is swinging in the other direction, quite possibly reinventing the conflict cycle in at least in a different form without moving towards reconciliation; whatever the remaining talk about reconciliation is due to the international pressure.

Actors of Extremism

The actors of extremism are those who assert one dimension of the national question against the other, on both sides of the divide, without compromising for a balance between the two, quite detrimental to the country's stability, democracy and development. Like the SLFP, the UNP has also been complicit at times of asserting the external dimension of the national question against the minority rights of the national question. Quite similarly, like the LTTE, the TNA has also been complicit at different times asserting the internal dimension of the national question quite detrimental to the external or the country dimension of the national question. But in relative terms, the UNP and the TNA are moderate forces that can be relied upon in bringing a compromised solution to the country. Even within the SLFP, there were moderate forces that were willing to compromise on the national question prior to the advent of Mahinda Rajapaksa to the leadership. The 'package' and the 2000 August draft constitution were some examples. Even there is an opportunistic deviation between the initial Mahinda Chinthana (i.e. 13+) and the post-Mahinda Chinthana policy of Mahinda Rajapaksa. What can be seen is the hardening of the extremist stance of the Rajapaksa administration on the national question day by day.

Some of the broad contours for a compromise on the two dimensions of the national question could be a political system based on a united country, autonomy and devolved powers, enshrined human and minority rights, multi-culturalism both in theory and practice, and institutionalized power sharing both at the center and the periphery as relevant. There is a need to understand the other side of the coin on the part of all protagonists and more and more efforts at assessing and evaluating the issues beyond one's own ethnicity or ethnic prism. Both academics and journalists (similar species) particularly need to see beyond their own ethnic affiliations.

Conclusion

Now one extreme to the political equation, the LTTE, is gone; the other still remains and that is the Rajapaksa administration. It is difficult to see a political resolution to the national question within this administration, although even after, the tasks might not be that smooth. At least a change might bring a manageable situation. There are so many other related and distinctly related matters why the Rajapaksa administration should go. Those are matters of democracy, good governance, imposed economic hardships, human rights, violence, corruption, and communalism, family-rule, rule of law or simple reasons of political decency. I have never seen a regime deteriorating into such low levels, like the present administration, within such a short pace of time.

What is necessary to bring about a political or a regime change is a broad collation of democratic forces both in the South and the North, at the beginning marching separately and striking together, and eventually forging more understanding and alliances for a viable Political Front even drawing upon the liberal and leftist sections within the present government itself.

(This article which might give a balanced perspective on the national question was first published in *The Island*, the *Asian Tribune*, the *Colombo Telegraph* and the *Sri Lanka Guardian* in June 2012. The *Daily Mirror* also reproduced it in an abridged form)

Laksiri Fernando

18

Making a Stop to Acrimonious 'Ethnic Debates'

"The hardest thing of all is to find a black cat in a dark room, especially if there is no cat." - Confucius

On 19 January a seminar was held in Jaffna organized by the Swiss Institute for Federalism of Fribourg, Switzerland, on the invitation of the Chief Minister of the Northern Province, C. V. Wigneswaran. The local partner of the seminar was the Institute for Constitutional Studies (ICS) in Colombo. When the Chief Minister's opening address was published in the Colombo Telegraph (20 January 2016), a rather acrimonious debate ensured in the form of comments and counter-comments. To be fair by the Swiss Institute, it should be stated that it is not an institute which advocates federalism for other countries, but believes that 'increasingly countries are incorporating elements of federalism into their structures in response to recent demands for increased regional autonomy and independence.' The Institute of Federalism is attached to the Faculty of Law of the University of Fribourg, Switzerland. Their focus is much wider and the following appears as the first paragraph of their 'About Us.'

The Institute of Federalism is recognized both nationally and internationally as a center of expertise in the field of governance. For nearly 30 years the Institute has been producing academic analyses of the responsibilities which lie with a government and of the conflicts of interest it faces in performing its tasks. These include fulfilling the duties of a government in line with needs but economically, acting in accordance with democratic legitimacy, taking the different sections of society into account and protecting the rights of individuals and minorities.

The Trigger

The trigger for the debate appears to be the following statement, among others, made by the Chief Minister and I am quoting a full paragraph.

Second fear expressed is that Sri Lanka is a Sinhala Buddhist country and the Tamils who are immigrants of recent yesteryears are asking more than they could and should. That is not so. History does not support the Mahawansa story. Also there is no ethnic group called the Sinhalese. The Sinhala language itself came into being only around 6th century AD. There was no Sinhala language before that. It is ideal to get a group of International Historians to investigate these facts. There is on the other hand contrary evidence of the existence of pre Buddhistic Hindu culture in the North and East available.

Even if I ignore his other utterances, there is a clear statement that "*there is no ethnic group called the Sinhalese*," a denial of the 'other.' There is a possibility that the CM was quite emotional at his address and his anger or acrimony led to the utterance. If that was the case, he should have carefully gone through the text and corrected or moderated it before sending it for publication. If that was a statement by an ordinary person or even an ordinary politician, it could have been ignored. However, the person is the Chief Minister of the Northern Province. The statement comes at a time when there is much hope that a New Constitution could be inaugurated and a greater or clear autonomy could be given to the Northern and the Eastern Provinces along with the other provinces.

Then there was an immediate retribution from one Vibhushana, someone using a pseudonym, claiming that even the Tamils in the North were "brought for road and rail construction not to be sent back to India but settled in isolation of the Sinhalese in Jaffna." It was claimed that the settlements were aimed at creating an exclusive Malabar region. There were other insults and the whole history was put upside down, like the Mahavamsa treatment by the CM. It is interesting to note that Vibhushana never came to the brawl thereafter.

Necessary Premises

It is a common sense premise to acknowledge that there should be 'mutual respect for each other' for any reconciliation between conflicting parties. It is more important in respect of an ethnic conflict. Referring to many conflicts in the former Yugoslavia, Franke Wilmer (*The Social Construction of Man, the State and War*, 2002) has said the following.

There are 4,000 to 5,000 ethnic or identity groups in the world, living in fewer than 200 states. Virtually all societies are multi-ethnic, and even those less so are in theory open to immigration and thus potentially more multi-ethnic in the future. Restructuring the basis of civic obligation within the state from one based on a perception of sameness to one of mutual respect, of reciprocity and interchangeability even in light of differences is not a moral luxury, it is a necessity. (p. 261).

There should be a change in 'man and woman' apart from restructuring of the state, to mean particularly constitutional changes at this stage. Not only rights, but also obligations should be emphasized. As Wilmer emphasized, restructuring or transforming 'the basis of civic obligation from one based on sameness to one of mutual respect is a necessity.' This is the same what was emphasized by the Organization for Security and Cooperation in Europe (OSCE) during particularly the Kosovo crisis. Their mission was as follows.

OSCE mission would be guided by the importance of bringing about mutual respect and reconciliation among all ethnic groups in Kosovo and of establishing a viable multi-ethnic society where the rights of each individual are fully and equally respected.

There is no attempt in this article to equate or compare Kosovo with Sri Lanka. But most of the principles applicable to many ethnic conflicts are common at the base. The details have to be worked out on that bases and above them. There shouldn't be any intolerance or even unease on the part of the Sinhalese, in my opinion, if and when Tamil political leaders articulate their traditional demand of 'federalism' or even the 'right to self-determination.' These can be and should be discussed in a rational or even a 'social-scientific' manner. At the same time, the Tamil leaders or the Sinhala leaders should not come up with 'outrageous' or 'farfetched' statements that can hamper a proper and a constructive dialogue. The obligations are not only for the leaders, but also for the general public, activists, journalists and the academics.

Acrimonious Debate

When Vibhushana made his 'outrageous' comments, a moderate Tamil opinion asked the question: "What is the compulsion that makes you write such nonsense?" While he was dismissing Vibhushana's claims as 'nonsense,' there was an admission that he must have been compelled by something which was in CM's statement. This highlights what is lacking in many 'ethnic debates' which should in fact be dialogues. If Vibhushana had pointed out what was wrong or disagreeable in Wigneswaran's statement, it could have been a constructive dialogue. But without that, it has led to an acrimonious debate.

There have been over 100 comments within two days and most of them were insulting communally, but not personally, thus escaped the 'guillotine' of the editors. Few were 'edited out' when they were clearly going beyond the guidelines. Some of the utterances were: 'Tamils are primitive and backward race,' 'Mahavamsa is crap... Sinhalaya Modaya!' I am not quoting full length of 'imprudence' not to aggravate the situation. Some of the postings appeared serious claims about history from both sides, but some others were simple fabrications just to annoy or frustrate 'the other.' Some referred to credible authorities on the subject of history, but often distorting them for their own arguments.

One James gave an elaborate explanation rather to justify Wigneswaran's theory that 'Sinhalese are not really an ethnicity.' The claim was that many present day 'Sinhalese' in the South had originated in South India, which in fact can be a fact. No ethnicity could claim purity. Claim for 'purity' or 'exclusivity' could be an inhibition for reconciliation from anyone's part. One 'Paul' asked, in my opinion correctly "How can the Tamils be a distinct people when every poster is claiming that the Sinhalese are from S. India or have Tamil origins or are Tamils themselves?" There were no insults or anything else in that positing. It is possible that some of the angry comments from the Tamil side came not only because of the past treatments or atrocities but also the new chauvinist trends like 'Sinha-Le.' However, none of them is a reason for Wigneswaran's irresponsible statements.

There were however saner comments or arguments mostly coming from those who were appearing in their own names. When using their own names and taking responsibility for what they say, naturally, there was some moderation and rationality. But most unfortunate was that some who began arguments rationally soon caving in for emotions and joining the bandwagon of bigotry. It is important to quote Dr Rajasingham Narendran who tried his best to give some sense to the debate and keep a balance. I am directly reproducing his comment only separating it into paragraphs.

Bigotry begets bigotry. Foolishness of old is being deliberately revived with intemperate, unnecessary and unwise words and similar responses. Where is the 'uniqueness' we are debating? Is it in our genes, conduct and thoughts?

"We speak related languages, eat the same food and practice related religions. We have more in common than most other people's. We have shared our foolishness several times over and paid a heavy price for this. We shared the pain too and have displayed similar bestiality. Modern genetic studies indicate that the indigenous Sinhalese and Tamils, have the same genetic base. Others have been invited-in, largely from South India and have become part of our mosaic.

Ultimately, all of us, including our aboriginal Veddas, stood up in East Africa and walked across to where we are now!

Please do not cook a Witch's brew once again foolishly, when some solutions to our problems are being contemplated and actively pursued. Any solutions that will solve our post-war problems and pave the way for our economic resurgence would be good solutions in the circumstances we are currently in."

CVW, you will be blamed and cursed by history, for paving the way to acrimony and its consequences once again with unwise words, phrases and concepts. You are, deliberately or inadvertently, becoming part of a curse that has bedeviled Sinhalese, Tamils and this island for decades now. You are kindling fires that that were subsiding but yet smoldering. There are many waiting to use your words as an excuse to pour oil on smoldering fires, from both sides of the rather fragile fence. It was not to play this role that you were nominated by the TNA and elected by an overwhelming majority!"

No further comment is necessary.

Some Lessons

It is intriguing how people are obsessed with 'history' and ready to inflame emotions on the basis of their 'bigoted history,' from both sides of the divide. It is my view that those who do so belong to a particular social milieu ('the bigoted leisure classes' I may say) and not the suffering general masses. Both or the obviously 'contradictory versions' of history cannot be true. History of the ancient past should be taken with equanimity today. Most important is to place our history in the broader context of human history.

It is a simple fact that our lives are connected to that of our parents and grandparents and so on through a web of familial, cultural, linguistic and religious traditions that is difficult to disentangle (Ludwig Wittgenstein).

That is how we have become who we are whether Sinhalese, Tamils or Muslims. Those are our identities which are also interwoven with each other through history, politics, economic interdependence and common living. However, the relative differences are no reason to fight each other or argue with each other in an acrimonious manner. Whatever Wigneswaran has stated, and whatever the retributory comments, those should not be utilized any longer to inflame emotions or create more controversies.

(The *Colombo Telegraph*, *The Island* and the *Sri Lanka Guardian* published this article in January 2016)

19
Building Inter-Ethnic 'Social Capital' for Reconciliation

"An association unites the energies of divergent minds and vigorously direct them toward a clearly indicated goal." – Alexis de Tocqueville

The need is true even in the case of the recent student clash at the University of Jaffna. Both Sinhala and Tamil students in the Science Faculty sat side by side, perhaps in two groups, in lecture halls and in science labs, interacting with their teachers vertically. But they hardly had horizontal connections among themselves. As Pratheep Kunarthnam writing on the subject asked, *"Can any of the authorities explain why except in one or two faculties Tamil-Sinhala students do not even smile at each other even when they walk past one another?"* (Colombo Telegraph, 20 July 2016). He also raised the question of 'deteriorating relations between Tamil and Muslim students.'

It is normal when people enter school, college, university or workplace, they tend to interact with their 'own people,' unless one or two 'enlightened souls' take a special effort to break the ice. In the case of Sri Lanka, most of these places are mono-cultural (not multi-cultural) spaces, most often purposely created that way. Even then they find reasons to group with their village or caste people. I am not touching on the gender issue here because of its 'sex-complexity,' although for a healthy society, healthy gender relations are necessary beyond marriage or partnership. Even if we consider humans as utterly 'autonomous' individuals, they do need grouping, socialization, interaction and net-works. When this happens within their own group or 'in-group,' it is generally called 'bonding.' That is how a society builds up 'social capital' for its survival and beyond. But in a multi-ethnic and a multi-religious society, there is something necessary beyond 'bonding' and towards 'bridging.' I am here borrowing simplified terminology and a conceptual framework from Robert Putnam and others on 'social capital formation' (*"Making Democracy Work,"* 1993).

A Conceptual Framework

How many 'mono-ethnic' societies or countries do we have today? The number is less than the number of our fingers. This is the reality in most countries that people have to face, whether you like it or not, and however much you argue about the predominance of your own group in your country or region. The building of 'social capital' is about networking for your personal and collective wellbeing, whether it is a funeral society, neighborhood association, temple/church organization, drama society or lending association. This is important as building physical capital, financial capital or human capital. At a higher level, you may have to build student associations, women's organizations, trade unions, human rights organizations, citizen's committees or even more politically overt social justice movements. These are important for an efficient and an effective democratic society. This may be accepted without much controversy. In general terms, the maturity of any democratic society could be judged or measured on the basis of the nature, the quality and the functions of these networks and associations which could also be called the civil society. If we wish a definition or an authoritative explanation on the matter, we can get it from Putnam, who was not the first to identify the phenomenon or process, but who was the first to elaborate, classify and use it as a criteria for assessing the maturity of democratic societies. As he said:

Of all the dimensions along which forms of social capital vary, perhaps the most important is the distinction between <u>bridging</u> (or inclusive) and <u>bonding</u> (or exclusive). Some forms of social capital are, by choice or necessity, inward looking and tend to reinforce exclusive identities and homogeneous groups. Examples of bonding social capital include ethnic fraternal organizations, church-based women's reading groups, and fashionable country clubs. Other networks are outward looking and encompass people across diverse social cleavages. Examples of bridging social capital include the civil rights movement, many youth service groups, and ecumenical religious organizations. (*Bowling Alone*, 2000, p. 23).

In the above work, Putnam was talking about the American situation ('The Collapse and Revival of American Community' as the sub-title), and his examples might not be the best for Sri Lanka. He did emphasize the importance of 'bridging' over 'bonding,' however the importance of 'bridging' is much more than he talked about, particularly in the case of Sri Lanka or any transitional or developing multi-cultural society. I am using the expressions 'transitional' and 'developing' both in economic and political terms.

Present Context

As generally accepted, there has been a resurgence of the civil society organizations (or networking) in Sri Lanka that led to or accompanied by the democratic change in 2015. This was not exactly the case five ten years ago - first due to the bitter civil war and then the authoritarian regime that emerged after the end of the war defeating the LTTE. In heralding the authoritarian development, there was a different or a 'primitive' kind of social capital or networking that emerged based on the 'kith and kin,' 'friendship alliances,' 'provincialism' and 'patron-client relations' that in fact effectively overturned the democratic fabric. This is popularly called the Rajapaksa regime. Primitive kind of social capital emerging out of traditional sources is also something anticipated by the social capital theorists. There can be several other forms of 'social capital' that could be inimical to justice and fairness. What made the democratic system barely saved was the resurrection of the nearly moribund civil society organizations (of lawyers, academics, professionals, journalists, students, citizens) and the emergence of new ones inspired largely by the international influence and civic consciousness. Two of the key objectives of the political change and thus the civil society were (1) the resurrection of democracy and (2) reconciliation of the ethnic conflict. I am not undermining the role of the political leaders or the political parties in the change, but emphasizing the importance of the civil society organizations for the purpose of this article.

The above was possible because of the long standing traditions of civil society organizations and networks in Sri Lanka although they became disrupted and degenerated during the period of the war and even before. First to breakdown, due to the ethnic distancing and antagonisms of the post-1956 period, were the processes of 'bridging social capital' in the country. Then came the disruption of even 'bonding social capital' primarily due to political interventions, war and demoralization of the civil society actors since 1983. The new forms in fact had emerged. Jonathan Goodhand, Hulme and Lewer (2000) have investigated some of the transformations in different zones. Even if we now assume - based on the democratic changes of the last year (2015), and still the vibrant activities of some of the organizations - that 'bonding social capital' is on track again, this article argues that 'bridging social capital' is still lagging behind which is much more important for the objectives of both 'resurrection of democracy' and 'building reconciliation' in the country.

Important Organizations

It might not be too arbitrary to identify the following organizations playing a major role in the recent democratic change in the country. They are listed in the alphabetical order.

> Bar Association of Sri Lanka (BASL)
> Centre for Policy Alternatives (CPA)
> Federation of University Teachers Associations (FUTA)
> Free Media Movement (FMM)
> National Movement for Social Justice (NMSJ)
> National Peace Council (NPC)
> People's Action for Free and Fair Elections (PAFFREL)
> Purawesi Balaya (People's Power)

Among them, while the NMSJ and the People's Power are new, or rather spontaneous, the others have had fairly a long standing existence in the country. The question which needs to be posed here however is whether they are only for 'bonding' or whether they have an objective for 'bridging.' 'Bonding' and 'bridging' or 'bonding social capital' and 'bridging social capital' are two different things particularly in terms of reconciliation after a conflict or war. While 'boding' tends to create networks within an in-group - within a particular ethnicity in this case – 'bridging' particularly means conscious efforts to transcend these barriers as a primary objective. No need to overemphasize such a need in Sri Lanka's context today, whether in the South, East or the North. A quick glance at the composition of the office bearers or the active leaders of the above organizations reveal that the CPA and the NPC undoubtedly have this 'bridging' quality at least at the decision making level. But both organizations are primarily located in Colombo, of course playing an advocacy (vertical) role. The BASL gives a symbolic prominence for the 'other ethnicity' and its office bearers understandably are elected ones. The PAFFREL is fairly represented in the Board of Directors but not in the Secretariat.

Being a past member, I can be more critical of the situation of FUTA only having a Vice-President at present from Jaffna! There cannot be any doubt that the academics could play an active role in 'bridging social capital' in theoretical terms, and through academic solidarity and cooperation. One way might be to resurrect the University Teachers for Human Rights (UTHR) also for Reconciliation (UTHR&R) island wide. The FMM is also primarily in the form of bonding. While the potential of both the NMSJ and the Peoples' Power (Purawesi Balaya) is so enormous in creating social capital in the country, transcending ethnic and religious divide, the present situation is almost completely confined to 'bonding.' Another important organization is the Citizens' Movement for Good Governance (CIMOGG), although its role in recent political change in practical terms is not readily verifiable (at least for me). However it has noble objectives very much similar to building 'social capital' even with a People Empowerment Programme (PEP).

Some Obstacles

While most of the obstacles that the civil society organizations are facing in moving beyond 'bonding' towards 'bridging' can be historical, there are certain ideological as well as practical reasons for the situation. When new organizations like the NMSJ or the Peoples Power are formed, it may be natural for them to begin within their known terrain. However, there should be some conscious efforts to move beyond. The past historical developments in the country, the state policies, terrorism and war have created enormous divisions even among the academics, professionals and social activists. There are unconscious inhibitions preventing joint work. These may be higher among the Tamils and the Muslims. A seemingly ideological reason for the situation seems to be that most of the organizations that recently sprung to oppose authoritarianism, or to bargain based on their demands, whether FUTA, NMSJ or Peoples Power, work on vertical lines trying to influence the new government and the leaders. Their demands may transcend ethnic or religious lines. They may also be fully committed to reconciliation in theoretical terms. But their 'vertical' approach trying mainly to 'influence the government' not only betray the purpose but also represents a compartmentalized elitism unless they venture to build most necessary 'bridging social capital' in the country. Another mindboggling question is 'why the hell' they don't coordinate each other and work together in achieving their seemingly similar objectives!

The task of building reconciliation is multi-faceted and require different track level interventions. The task of 'bridging social capital' is a task primarily for the civil society. It cannot be expected from the political leaders. Political leaders of any country are strange animals. They changes 'color' after power like chameleons. The formation of 'bridging social capital' in society entails not only networking or forming multi-ethnic organizations. It is also a task of education, attitudinal change and building necessary skills. One practical difficulty, among others, is the language barrier between the Sinhala speakers and the Tamil speakers. The promotion of English as the link language has not progressed well even in university education. However, to reach the broader sections of the people, the civil society organizations have to work both in Sinhala and Tamil, apart from English. This should be followed as a cardinal principle. That is the only way to attract 'the other' and create conditions for 'bridging,' whether your present base is Sinhalese, Tamil or Muslim. This is something terribly lacking in the present popular organizations.

Given the fact that most or almost all prominent organizations are Colombo based, and the emergence of such organizations in Jaffna or in the North/East were largely inhibited due to the war devastation, the failure of the present organizations to work in Tamil has been a major setback for 'bridging social capital' formation even after a democratic change last year. This is a major obstacle for ethnic reconciliation in the country as at present. The formation of social capital in Sri Lanka, linked to economy and polity and also in the context of ethnic conflict, is undoubtedly an area that needs new research by young academics. While Robert Putnam and David Halpern are some theoretical pioneers in this field, Jonathan Goodhand and N. Uphoff with C. M. Wijayaratna have some empirical observations on Sri Lanka (See Bibliography).

(*The Island,* the *Colombo Telegraph* and the *Sri Lanka Guardian* previously published this article in August 2016)

SELECTED BIBLIOGRAPHY

Achcar, Gilbert. 2013. *Marxism, Orientalism, Cosmopolitanism*. London: Saqi Books.

Amerasinghe, Ranjith et al (Ed.). 2011. *Twenty Years of Devolution: An Evaluation of the Working of Provincial Councils in Sri Lanka*. Colombo: Institute for Constitutional Studies.

Anderson, Perry. 1974. *Lineages of the Absolutist State*. London: Verso.

Ardent, Hannah. 1958. *The Origins of Totalitarianism*. New York: Meridian.

Ardent, Hannah. 1963. *On Revolution*. New York: Viking Press.

Athukorala, Premachandra and S. Jayasuriya. 2015. "Victory in War and Defeat in Peace: Politics and Economics of Post-Conflict Sri Lanka." *Asian Economic Papers* 14(3).

Bandarage, Asoka. 2009. *The Separatist Conflict in Sri Lanka: Terrorism, Ethnicity, Political Economy*. New York: Routledge.

Beetham, David and Kevin Boyle. 2009. *Introducing Democracy*. Paris: UNESCO.

Bohman, J. and M. Lutz-Bachmann (Eds.). 1997. *Perpetual Peace: Essays on Kant's Cosmopolitan Ideal*. Massachusetts: MIT Press.

Caramani, Daniele. (Ed). 2014. *Comparative Politics*. Oxford: Oxford University Press.

Chandraprema, C. A. 2012. *Gota's War*. Colombo: Ranjan Wijeratne Foundation.

De Silva, K. M. 1986. *Religion, Nationalism, and the State in Modern Sri Lanka*. Florida: University of South Florida.

De Tocqueville, Alexis. 2004. *Democracy in America*. New York: Library Classics.

De Visser, J. W. 2005. *Developmental Local Government: A Case Study of South Africa*. Oxford: Antwerpen.

DeVotta, Neil. 2004. *Blowback: Linguistic Nationalism, Institutional Decay and Ethnic Conflict in Sri Lanka*. Stanford: Stanford University Press.

DeVotta, Neil. 2014. *From Civil War to Soft Authoritarianism: Ethnonationalism and Democratic Regression in Sri Lanka*. New York: Routledge.

Delanty, G. and K. Kumar (Eds.). 2006. *The Sage Handbook of Nations and Nationalism*. London: Sage.

Delanty, G. 2009. *The Cosmopolitan Imagination: The Renewal of Critical Social Theory*. Cambridge: Cambridge University Press.

Delanty, G. (Ed.). 2012. *Routledge Handbook of Cosmopolitanism Studies*. New York: Routledge.

Elazar, Daniel. 1995. *Federalism Theory and Application Vol. 1*. Pretoria: HSRC Publications.

Evans, Gareth. 2008. *Responsibility to Protect: Ending Mass Atrocity Crimes Once and for All*. Washington: Brookings Institution Press.

Fernando, Basil. 2012. "Sri Lanka: The Need to Re-interpret the Executive President's Impunity under Article 35 (1)." Hong Kong: Asian Human Rights Commission.

Fernando, Laksiri. 1988. "The Challenge of the Open Economy: Trade Unionism in Sri Lanka" in Roger Southall (Ed.). *Trade Unions and New Industrialization of the Third World*. London: Zed Press.

Fernando, Laksiri and Dietmar Kneitschel. 1999. *A New Electoral System for Sri Lanka?* Colombo: FES.

Fernando, Laksiri. 2002. *Human Rights, Politics and States: Burma, Cambodia and Sri Lanka*. Colombo: SSA.

Fernando, Laksiri. 2005. *Police-Civil Relations for Good Governance*. Colombo: SSA.

Fernando, Laksiri. 2007. "Sri Lanka's Predicament: Ethno-Nationalism versus Civic-Nationalism,*"Asian Tribune* (25 June 2007).

Fernando, Laksiri Fernando. 2013. "Sri Lanka: On the Question of Nationalism." *Colombo Telegraph* (13 May 2013).

Fernando, Laksiri. 2015. "A Victory for 'Cosmopolitanism' over Narrow Nationalism." *Sri Lanka Guardian* (29 August 2015).

Garner, Robert et al. 2012. *Introduction to Politics*. Oxford: Oxford University Press.

Ghai, Yash and Jill Cottrell (Ed). 2004. *Economic, Social and Cultural Rights in Practice*. London: Interights.

Goodhand, Jonathan et al. 2000. "Social Capital and the Political Economy of Violence: A Case Study of Sri Lanka.*" Disasters* 24 (4).

Goonewardene, Leslie. 1980. *A New Road is Needed*. Colombo: IGM Ltd.

Gunasinghe, Newton. 2004. "The Open Economy and Its Impact on Ethnic Relations in Sri Lanka" in Deborah Winslow and Michael D. Woost, *Economy, Culture and Civil War in Sri Lanka*. Bloomington: Indiana University Press.

Gunawardene, Nalaka. 2015. "Sri Lankan Parliamentary Election 2015: How Did Social Media Make A Difference?" *Groundviews* (3 September 2015).

Halpern, David. 2005. *Social Capital*. Cambridge: Polity Press.

Hasbullah, S. H. and Barrie M. Morrison (Ed.). 2004. *Sri Lankan Society in an Era of Globalization*. London: Sage.

Held, David (Ed). 2010. *Cosmopolitanism: Ideals, Realities & Deficits*. Cambridge: Polity Press.

Hobsbawm, Eric. 1990. *Nations and Nationalism since 1780: Programme, Myth, Reality*. Cambridge: Cambridge University Press.

Horowitz, Donald. 2001. *The Deadly Ethnic Riot.* Berkeley: University of California Press.

Huntington, Samuel P. 1984. "Will More Countries Become Democratic?" *Political Science Quarterly* 99 (2).

Hurley, S. L. 1999. "Rationality, Democracy and Leaky Boundaries: Vertical vs. Horizontal Modularity," *Journal of Political Philosophy* 7 (2).

Hyndman, Patricia. 1992. *Human Rights Accountability in Sri Lanka.* New York: Human Rights Watch.

Jalal, Ayesha. 1995. *Democracy and Authoritarianism in South Asia: A Comparative and Historical Perspective.* Massachusetts: Harvard University Press.

Jayatilleka, Dayan. 2016. "Weakening the Centre through Covert Federalsim," *Colombo Telegraph* (1 September).

Jayawickrema, Nihal. 1976. *Human Rights in Sri Lanka.* Berkeley: University of California.

Jayewardene, J. R. 1974. *Selected Speeches, 1944-1973.* Colombo: H. W. Cave.

Jennings, Ivor. 1953. *The Constitution of Ceylon,* Bombay: Oxford University Press.

Jupp, James. 1978. *Sri Lanka: Third World Democracy.* London: Frank Cass.

Kearney, Robert. 1967. *Communalism and Language in the Politics of Ceylon.* Durham: Duke University Press.

Kearney, Robert. 1985. "Ethnic Conflict and the Tamil Separatist Movement in Sri Lanka." *Asian Survey* 25 (9).

Keethaponcalan, S. I. 2009. *Conflict and Peace in Sri Lanka: Major Documents.* Colombo: Kumaran Book House.

Kedourie, Elie. 1960. *Nationalism.* London: Hutchinson.

Kleingeld, P. 2012. *Kant and Cosmopolitanism: The Philosophical Ideal of World Citizenship.* Cambridge: Cambridge University Press.

Kodikara, S. U. 1965. *Indo-Ceylon Relations since Independence.* Colombo: Ceylon Institute of World Affairs.

Kohn, Hans. 1944. *The Idea of Nationalism: The Study of Its Origins and Background.* New York: The Macmillan Publishers.

Lamparello, Adam. 2013. "Restoring Constitutional Equilibrium." *Social Science Research Network* (December).

Leach, Philip et al. 2010. *Responding to Systemic Human Rights Violations.* New York: Angus and Robertson.

Leitan, G. R. T. 1979. *Local Government and Decentralized Administration in Sri Lanka.* Colombo: Lake House.

Lerner, Hanna. 2011. *Making Constitutions in Deeply Divided Societies.* Cambridge: Cambridge University Press.

Murray, Nancy. 1984. "The State against Tamils," *Race & Class,* XXVI (1).

Nairn, Tom. 2003. *Break-up of Britain: Crisis and Neo-Nationalism.* Altona: Common Ground.

Perera, N. M. 1979. *Critical Analysis of the New Constitution of the Sri Lankan Government.* Colombo: V. S. Raja.

Putnam, Robert et al. 1993. *Making Democracy Work: Civic Traditions in Modern Italy.* Princeton: Princeton University Press.

Putnam, Robert. 2000. *Bowling Alone: The Collapse and Revival of American*

Community. New York: Simmon & Schuster.

Putnam, Robert (Ed.). 2002. *Democracies in Flux: The Evolution of Social Capital in Contemporary Society.*" Oxford: Oxford University Press.

Rajan, Theva. 1995. *Tamil as Official Language: Retrospect and Prospect.* Colombo: ICES.

Rupesinghe, Kumar and Berth Verstappen. 1989. *Ethnic Conflict and Human Rights in Sri Lanka: An Annotated Bibliography.* Oslo: Hans Zell.

Samaranayake, Gamini. 2007. *Political Violence in Sri Lanka, 1971-1978.* New Delhi: Gyan Books.

Sen, Amartya. 1999. *Development as Freedom.* Oxford: Oxford University Press.

Sheehan, Colleen. 2015. *The Mind of James Madison: The Legacy of Classical Republicanism.* Cambridge: Cambridge University Press.

Shue, Henry. 1980. *Basic Rights: Subsistence, Affluence and U.S. Foreign Policy.* Princeton: Princeton University Press.

Shugart, Matthew and John M. Carey. 1992. *Presidents and Assemblies.* Cambridge: Cambridge University Press.

Siverajah, Ambalavanar. 1996. *Politics of Tamil Nationalism in Sri Lanka.* New Delhi: South Asian Books.

Skogly, Sigrun. 2006. *Beyond National Borders: State's Human Rights Obligations in International Cooperation.* Oxford: Intersentia.

Sondgrass. Donald. 1966. *Ceylon: An Export Economy in Transition.* Homewood: R. D. Irwin.

Spagnoli, Filip. 2003. *Homo Democraticus: On the Universal Desirability and the Not So Universal Possibility of Democracy and Human Rights.* Buckinghamshire: Cambridge Scholars Press.

Temperman, Jeroen. 2010. *State-Religion Relationships and Human Rights Law.* Leiden: Martinus Nijhoff.

Uphoff, N. and C. M. Wijayaratna. 2000. "Demonstrated Benefits from Social Capital: The Productivity of Farmer Organizations in Gal Oya, Sri Lanka." *World Development* 28

Vasak, Karel (Ed.). 1982. *The International Dimensions of Human Rights* (Vol. 1 & 2). Paris: UNESCO.

Vertovec, S. and R. Cohen (Eds.). 2002. *Conceiving Cosmopolitanism: Theory, Context, and Practice.* Oxford: Oxford University Press.

Vittachi, Tarzie. 1958. *Emergency '58: The Story of the Ceylon Race Riots.* London: Andre Deutsch.

Watts, Duncan. 2003. *Understanding US/UK Government and Politics.* Manchester University Press.

Weerawardena, I. D. S. 1951. *The Government and Politics in Ceylon, 1931-1946.* Colombo: Economic Research Association.

Weerawardena, I. D. S. 1955. *The Senate of Ceylon at Work.* Peradeniya: University of Ceylon.

Welikala, Asanga (Ed). 2015 *Reforming Sri Lankan Presidentialism: Provenance, Problems and Prospects.* Colombo: Centre for Policy Alternatives.

Welikala, Asanga (Ed), 2016. *The Nineteenth Amendment to the Constitution.* Colombo: Centre for Policy Alternatives.

Wickramaratne, Jayampathy. 1996. *Fundamental Rights in Sri Lanka*. New Delhi: Navrang.

Wilmer, Franke. 2004. *The Social Construction of Man, the State and War*. New York: Routledge.

Wilson, A. J. 1980. *The Gaullist System in Asia: The Constitution of 1978*. London: Macmillan.

Wilson, A. J. 1988. *The Break-Up of Sri Lanka: The Sinhalese-Tamil Conflict*. London: C. Hurst.

Wilson, A. J. 2000. *Sri Lanka Tamil Nationalism*. London: C. Hurst.

Wittfogel, Karl. 1967. *Oriental Despotism: A Comparative Study of Total Power*. London: Yale University Press.

Wriggins, Howard. 1960. *Ceylon: Dilemmas of a New Nation*. Princeton: Princeton University Press.

REPORTS/MONOGRAPHS

Asian Human Rights Commission (AHRC). 2011. "A Review of Sri Lanka's Compliance with the Obligations under CAT." Hong Kong: AHRC.

Centre for Monitoring Election Violence (CMEV). 2010. "Final Report on Election Related Violence and Malpractices, Parliamentary Election 2010." Colombo: CMEV.

Commonwealth Expert Team. 2010. "Report of Sri Lanka Presidential Election, 26 January 2010." London: Commonwealth Secretariat.

Fernando, Ruki. 2010. "Key challenges of democratization in post war and post-election in Sri Lanka" (monograph). Colombo: Law and Society Trust.

International Crisis Group (ICG). 2010. "The Sri Lankan Tamil Diaspora after the LTTE," Asia Report 186, February 2010.

Public Representation Committee. 2016. "Report on Public Representation on Constitutional Reform." Colombo: www.yourconstitution.lk

Satkunanathan, Ambika. [No date] "Working of Democracy in Sri Lanka," (Monograph). Colombo: Law and Society Trust. http://www.democracy-asia.org/qa/srilanka/Ambika

UNDP. 2012. "Sri Lanka Human Development Report 2012." Colombo: UNDP Office.

United Nations. 2011. "Report of the Secretary-General's Panel of Experts on Accountability in Sri Lanka." New York: www.un.org/News/dh/infocus/Sri_Lanka/POE_Report_Full.pdf

(This Bibliography includes only the sources cited in the text, nevertheless gives a wide ranging theoretical and empirical studies relevant to the subject of new constitution making in Sri Lanka)

ABOUT THE AUTHOR

Laksiri Fernando (BA, Ceylon; MA, New Brunswick; and Ph. D, Sydney) is a published author with a long standing experience internationally and in Sri Lanka. He has held the positions of Senior Professor in Political Science and Public Policy, University of Colombo; Dean of the Faculty of Graduate Studies (FGS), University of Colombo; Director of the Centre for the Study of Human Rights (CSHR), University of Colombo; Chairperson and Director, Sri Lanka National Centre for Advanced Studies (NCAS); Director of the Sri Lanka Foundation Institute (SLFI); Secretary for Asia/Pacific of the World University Service (WUS Geneva); and Executive Director, Diplomacy Training Program (DTP), University of New South Wales, Australia, among others. He has been a Japan Foundation Scholar and has served as Visiting Scholar/Professor at the Universities of New South Wales, Australia; University of Heidelberg, Germany; Ryukoku University, Japan; and the University of Sydney, Australia. He has published many scholarly reviewed articles in journals, nationally and internationally. He now lives in Sydney, Australia, on retirement. He contributes regularly to printed and electronic newspapers and journals nationally and internationally that includes the *Sri Lanka Guardian*, *The Island* newspaper and the *Colombo Telegraph* among others.

OTHER BOOKS BY THE AUTHOR

Thomas More's Socialist Utopia and Ceylon (Sri Lanka)

Sri Lanka: Challenges of a Society in Transition (Edited)

Sri Lanka's Ethnic Conflict in the Global Context (Edited)

Political Science Approach to Human Rights

A New Electoral System for Sri Lanka (Edited)

Police-Civil Relations for Good Governance

Human Rights, Politics and States: Burma, Cambodia and Sri Lanka

Academic Freedom 1990: A Human Rights Report (Edited)

Jathika Viyaparaya, Viyawastha Wardanaya and Vamansika Viyaparaye Upatha